The American Revolution

the
FRENCH ALLIES

by Robin McKown

Illustrated with photographs and maps

McGRAW-HILL BOOK COMPANY

New York • Toronto • London • Sydney

For Hilda and Arthur

We are grateful for permission to reproduce photographs on the following pages:

6, 8, 12, 13, 20, 21 (bottom), 24, 34, 35, 45, 47, 50, 54, 56, 61, 87, 88 (top), and 91, courtesy The Library of Congress

11, 14 (bottom), and 15, courtesy the National Gallery of Art, Washington, D.C., Samuel H. Kress Collection

14 (top), and 92, courtesy The Mount Vernon Ladies' Association

16, 21 (top), 55, and 90 (top), courtesy The New York Public Library

22, 23, 36, 59, 74, and 82, courtesy United States George Washington Bicentennial Commission

26, 40, and 41, courtesy of The Metropolitan Museum of Art

27, 32, 37, 68, and 78, courtesy U. S. Signal Corps

28 and 29, courtesy French Cultural Services

31, 33 (top), 80, 81, 83, and 88 (bottom), courtesy National Park Service

42 and 94, photographs by Abbie Rowe—courtesy National Park Service

jacket and pages 33 (bottom), 38, 52, 64, 70, 84, 85, and 90 (bottom), courtesy Minor Congressional Commissions

39 and 75, courtesy the Virginia Department of Conservation and Development

49 and 51, courtesy U. S. Information Service

67 and 73, courtesy U. S. Naval Academy Museum

77, courtesy the Mariners Museum, Newport News, Va.

Library of Congress Catalog Card Number: 68-58211

1234567890 HDBP 754321069

Table of Contents

Other Books By Robin McKown

Nonfiction

THE CONGO: RIVER OF MYSTERY
HEROIC NURSES
THE STORY OF THE INCAS
BENJAMIN FRANKLIN
THOMAS PAINE
WASHINGTON'S AMERICA
ROOSEVELT'S AMERICA
ELEANOR ROOSEVELT'S WORLD
THE FABULOUS ISOTOPES
MARIE CURIE
GIANT OF THE ATOM: ERNEST RUTHERFORD
SHE LIVED FOR SCIENCE: IRÈNE JOLIOT-CURIE
MENDELEYEV AND HIS PERIODIC TABLE
SEVEN FAMOUS TRIALS

Fiction

THE BOY WHO WOKE UP IN MADAGASCAR
PATRIOT OF THE UNDERGROUND
JANINE
THE ORDEAL OF ANNE DEVLIN
RAKOTO AND THE DRONGO BIRD
GIRL OF MADAGASCAR

Preface

In the American Revolution, France played a vital role. Without French aid in men, money, and supplies, it is certain victory would have taken longer; it is even possible there would have been no victory.

In granting this aid, self-interest motivated the French rulers. The king of France and his ministers sought revenge on their ancient enemy, England. The people of France, a very large number of them, supported the American struggle against tyranny through pure idealism.

A curious paradox resulted. The self-interest of the rulers proved a boomerang. The monarchy of France collapsed, bankrupt by its American expenditures. The French people, infiltrated with ideas of freedom and democracy wafted from America, made their own revolution.

It is the idealism behind the French aid, not the self-interest, that has survived. The feeling it engendered was symbolized in the words uttered in the First World War, "Lafayette, we are here!" It created a warm and tangible bond that over the years has transcended politics and prejudice.

This is the story of the French participants in America's fight for independence, what they did and how and why.

Robin McKown

Marie Antoinette, queen of France

The Unlikely Allies

Colonies are like fruit which fall from a tree on ripening. When colonies become self-sufficient, they do as Carthage did, as America will one day do.
—Baron de Turgot, *French statesman, 1750*

On May 10, 1774, King Louis XV of France died of smallpox at the age of sixty-four in his palace at Versailles. His nineteen-year-old grandson, the dauphin who would henceforth be Louis XVI, knelt in the palace chapel in anguish.

"Oh, my God, what misfortune!" he cried out. "Oh, my God, help me!"

His wife, Marie Antoinette, knelt at his side, sobbing. "Oh God, guide us, protect us, we are so young!" She was only eighteen and very pretty. Soon she would forget her grief in her delight at being queen of France and indulging her taste in gowns and jewels and costly entertainment.

Her husband, a slow-thinking, awkward, earnest youth, did not want to rule France at all. His tastes were simple. He was passionately fond of hunting. He was an amateur locksmith and preferred tinkering in his workshop to attending state ceremonies. Although he was not brilliant, nor even clever, he was far from stupid. Since childhood he had read widely, particularly history, and his memory was excellent. Moreover, he was honest and virtuous and sincerely wanted to help his people.

On the first day of his reign he ordered that 200,000 livres (a livre was about twenty cents) be distributed to the poor of Paris. He refused the "Joyous Ascension" tax of 20,000,000 livres allotted to new monarchs, and he freed all serfs on the Crown lands.

His subjects went wild with joy. They were convinced that a new era of justice and prosperity lay ahead. That the king could not live up to their expectations was not due to lack of good intentions but to a fatal weakness in his character. He did not have the will power to stand by his convictions, even when he knew he was right.

To reduce the national deficit, which had mounted to large proportions during the reign of his indolent and pleasure-loving grandfather, the king appointed a seasoned statesman,

Destruction of the tea at Boston Harbor.

the Baron de Turgot, as finance minister. The baron, a capable man of great integrity, set in motion reforms to reduce government spending and the royal household expenses. He did not last. Marie Antoinette, indignantly accusing him of penny-pinching, led the protests against his economies. When Louis XVI yielded to pressure and signed the order for his dismissal, he murmured unhappily, "Only Monsieur Turgot and I love the people."

As his new foreign minister, the king appointed Charles Gravier, Comte de Vergennes. Vergennes was a shrewd, cautious, and polished diplomat of many years experience in foreign courts. His manner toward his youthful sovereign was as respectful as protocol demanded, but henceforth it was he, not the king, who made all decisions on foreign policy.

France was an absolute monarchy. Theoretically, Louis XVI had unlimited power. He never learned to make use of it. His inability to resist domination by his foreign minister would affect the destiny of America, a far land he would never see.

John Adams

In America, on April 19, 1775, less than a year after Louis XVI became king of France, shots were exchanged at Concord Bridge. Colonial militiamen carrying ancient muskets fought well-armed British Redcoats sent from Boston by General Thomas Gage to search Concord for military supplies. By all standards it was a minor clash. Eight British soldiers were killed and two Americans. The significance of the Battle of Concord Bridge was that it marked the opening of the American Revolution.

News of the first open rebellion of England's American colonists reached France by sailing ship, long after the event. Officially, Foreign Minister Vergennes expressed his sympathy to the English Ambassador in Paris, Lord Stormont. "The spirit of revolt, in whatever spot it breaks out, is always a dangerous precedent," he wrote. "It is with moral as with physical diseases, both may become contagious." His words expressed the sentiments of Louis XVI. Almost from infancy he had been instilled with a belief in the divine right of kings,

8

and he logically saw an uprising against any monarch as a threat to the whole structure of society.

In actual fact, Vergennes and many other French statesmen were secretly delighted. The chance that the American rebellion might spread seemed very remote. What was certain was that England was in serious trouble, as French observers had predicted years before.

England had defeated France badly in the Seven Years' War (1756–1763). In spite of the tenuous truce that now existed between the two countries, the humiliation of that defeat still rankled. By the 1763 Treaty of Paris, England had taken over Canada and other French territorial possessions in North America.

At the time, Foreign Minister Choiseul, under Louis XV, had warned a British statesman that England was making a mistake. So long as Canada was in French hands, he pointed out, it served to keep the colonies "in a state of dependence" on English support, but once it was ceded to England the colonies would not fail to free themselves. (John Adams of Massachusetts said much the same thing in different words. He bragged that once the "turbulent Gauls" were driven from Canada, "all Europe will be powerless to subjugate us.")

Washington taking command of the army at Cambridge.

The British refused to heed such warnings. Instead Parliament had tried to impose new taxes on the Americans and resorted to high-handed tactics to keep order. Over the years France sent spies to America to talk to people and find out how they felt about England. In 1768, the Prussian-born Baron Johann de Kalb, in the service of Louis XV, reported back that though there was some discontent, the American colonists were still loyal to the British Crown. The discontent had swollen mightily since then until, with the fighting at Concord, matters reached the point of no return.

The French had reason to feel complacent. By yielding Canada to England, they had managed to keep their islands in the West Indies, which paid enormous revenues from sugar and indigo plantations worked by African slave labor. Canada had never been a profitable venture. Underestimating its vast unexploited wealth, the satiric Voltaire summed it up as a land of "bears, beavers, and barbarians" and said that France was well rid of it. Now everything was working out as they had hoped. England was on the verge of a war with her distant colonies which might well prove long and costly and seriously drain her resources. Louis XVI had to agree with his foreign minister that it was not at all unpleasant to watch this happen, provided of course that France did not become involved. More than anything else, the king wanted to keep his country at peace.

The close check France was keeping on their activities would have surprised most Americans. France had been their enemy in the French and Indian War (a prelude to the Seven Years' War in Europe), in which, side by side with British soldiers, American militiamen had driven the French out of the Ohio valley and back to Canada. A certain prejudice against France also existed for religious reasons. Most of the American colonists were Protestant, whereas France was a Catholic country. During the reign of Louis XIV, many French Huguenots (Protestants) had fled to America to escape persecution. In general, France was regarded with suspicion and not with friendship. Nothing seemed more unlikely than that they would ever join forces.

Far more than the wide blue expanses of the Atlantic separated France and the thirteen colonies who paid allegiance to England. There were immense differences in their way of life, their way of thinking. France was a populous country of 25,000,000 with a civilization dating back for centuries. America had belonged to the Indians until a hundred and fifty years before. Most of it still did. The colonies along the eastern seaboard were sparsely settled with less than three million population. The vast wilderness to the west had hardly been explored at all.

Even under the domination of England, the colonists had long had a definite, if limited, say in their own government. Seven colonies were ruled by royal governors appointed by the British Crown, while the rest operated under special charters. All had provincial legislatures, usually composed of an upper house, appointed by the Crown or governor, and a lower house, elected by the people, though only men with property were allowed to vote. In many small towns, especially in New England, town meetings were held to decide on such local matters as the building of schools and the care of the aged and infirm.

In France, an absolute monarchy, there were no elections. Public officials were appointed by the king, often for reasons other than ability. It was possible to buy openly a judgeship and other official and semiofficial posts. America was the New World, struggling and striving. France was the Old World where patterns of greed and corruption had hardened, as Louis XVI discovered to his sorrow.

The greatest inequities existed between the upper and lower classes. Nobles and clergy were exempt from paying taxes. The heavy burden of taxation, in money, produce, or forced

A French peasant's home.

11

labor, fell upon the poor. (The independent Americans resented even the smallest tax imposed by the British Parliament.) While French peasants ate black bread, wore rags, and lived in hovels, the nobles dressed in silks and satins and powdered wigs and dined on gourmet foods.

There were approximately 80,000 noble families in France. The most eminent traced their ancestry back to ancient feudal kingdoms. There were also newcomers to the aristocracy. The king had the right to make nobles out of commoners for whatever reasons he chose.

The highest title, next to the king, was prince. In order of rank then came duke, marquis, count, viscount, baron, and knight. (In French, duke, count, viscount, and knight translate as *duc, comte, vicomte,* and *chevalier.*) The most privileged stayed at Versailles as courtiers, where they could attend the functions of a court so splendid it was known as the "Sun Kingdom."

With few exceptions, the only careers open to the nobility were in the church and the military. (All army and navy officers had to be of noble birth.) Many of the nobility, men and women both, were persons of culture and intelligence but their abilities were largely wasted. To their credit they patronized the arts.

In matters of taste and culture, France was not only in advance of the colonies but led all other European countries. Throughout the Continent, French was the language of the upper classes. Dolls dressed in the latest Paris fashions were

A well-to-do American woman arrives at a colonial Christmas Eve celebration.

sent by French dressmakers as models for foreign capitals. For reasons of prestige, European nobility furnished their mansions with French furniture, bought French art and sculpture, hired French cooks. German princes ruined themselves in building imitations of the palace of Versailles. Foreign kings tried to lure French writers to their courts, promising them pensions and freedom from censor.

A New England kitchen in 1776.

America had a scattering of scholars, several universities, and a number of fine craftsmen, but had hardly had time to develop a heritage of art, literature, and music. It had its rich and its poor, but the rich were not so extravagant as their French counterparts, nor were the poor so wretched. The French officer, the Comte de Ségur, was impressed "by the entire absence of the extremes both of opulence and misery" in America, by the houses, "clean, elegant, painted in bright and varied colors, and standing in little gardens behind pretty fences," and by the inhabitants, who "exhibited the unassuming and quiet pride of men who have no masters."

For everyone in America, the cardinal virtues were thrift and hard work. America was a land of opportunity for those willing to use their hands and their skills. Such opportunity was lacking in France. If peasants showed signs of well-being, it only made the tax collectors more greedy.

Well-to-do American women took their household chores as seriously as the wives of farmers. General George Washington's wife, Martha, rose at dawn to supervise the laundry, smokehouse, dairy, and kitchen at their prosperous Virginia plantation of Mount Vernon. In her leisure hours, she instructed her children in reading, writing, music, and dancing.

Upper-class French women left household matters to their servants and children to their tutors. The frivolous spent their days with their hairdresser and dressmaker and their nights at balls and gaming tables. The more serious followed intellectual pursuits. The Marquise du Châtelet, an intimate friend of Voltaire, was a scientist who made an admirable French translation of the works of Sir Isaac Newton.

In Paris, there were noblewomen, usually elderly and always distinguished, whose main occupation was holding weekly salons, to which they invited the most important, brilliant, and controversial personages in Europe. For the bored aristocracy, such gatherings furnished stimulation they could find nowhere else. In the salons, dangerous ideas— that is, ideas which the government considered dangerous— were freely discussed.

13

Martha Washington

Voltaire

While freedom of the press was well established in America, in France the king could ban any literary work that displeased him and exile or imprison the author. Forbidden books were frequently burned by the public executioner. No risk or danger could stop writers from writing what they thought. To elude the censor, they cloaked their stories in allegory, used pseudonyms, or published their works in neighboring countries and had them smuggled into France. Books on controversial themes always found a wide audience and were read with delight, especially by the aristocracy they so often criticized. Their contents made juicy conversation in the fashionable salons of Paris.

The philosopher and scholar Baron de Montesquieu (1689–1755), who had observed French society during the reigns of both Louis XIV and Louis XV, used an imaginative device to point out its foibles in his *Persian Letters*. Through the eyes of two distinguished Persian travelers, Montesquieu describes eighteenth-century Paris, with its pleasures, absurdities, and inconsistencies. France is a country where "they are fond of defending extraordinary opinions." "A great noble is a man who sees the king, speaks to the ministers, who has ancestors, debts, and pensions." The king has "more statues in his palace garden [Versailles] than there are citizens in a large town." Often he gives higher rewards to the obsequious courtier who hands him a napkin at his table than to the general who wins battles for him. He is a "great magician" who puts it into men's heads that a piece of paper is money!

Montesquieu expanded his ideas on government in a later and more celebrated work, *The Spirit of the Laws*. There were three major types of government, he said: tyranny, based on fear; democracy, which to function successfully must rely on the civic virtue of the majority of its citizens; and monarchy, which depended on the principle of honor. Of the three, he professed to favor monarchy, not the absolute monarchy existing in France, but one in which the power of the king was offset by independent judicial and legislative bodies, similar to the British parliamentary system, which he admired with certain reservations.

Montesquieu's books went into many editions and were still widely read and quoted. His popularity extended as far away as Russia and America.

Among living French authors, Voltaire (1694–1778) was conceded to be the greatest. Witty, caustic, with a golden gift of words, he was constantly in trouble with the government or the Church. For a satire which was actually at-

14

tributed to him falsely, he was at one time imprisoned in the Bastille. Again and again he fled to the provinces or out of the country to escape the wrath of the censors. Yet whenever he risked returning to Paris, women of high society vied with one another for the honor of entertaining him.

The scholar Denis Diderot (1713–1784) edited a massive encyclopedia designed "to build a genealogical tree of all human knowledge." Famous writers, scientists, religious authorities, and experts in all fields contributed articles. There were articles by workmen on the techniques of their trades. Twice publication was suspended by royal decree. Permission to issue the heavy volumes was granted, in 1772, only after the king of Prussia and the empress of Russia both offered to publish them in their own countries. Diderot and his writers, known as the Encyclopedists, were largely responsible for creating an atmosphere where rational thinking could triumph over superstition and prejudice.

The dancer La Camargo entertains the French aristocracy.

Perhaps the most influential writer in France during the early years of the rule of Louis XVI was Jean-Jacques Rousseau (1712–1788), who was Swiss by birth, and whose own unhappy childhood and youth led to his deep concern with social injustice. "Man is born free and everywhere is enslaved," he wrote. "There is no such thing as a justifiable government resting on force alone." Man was naturally good, he theorized, but society had corrupted him. The only course to follow was to flee society and live in the woods as simply as a peasant.

This idea of returning to nature had a tremendous appeal for nobles accustomed to the artificial court life of Versailles. America seemed to them the primeval paradise Rousseau had in mind. The wave of sympathy that was to sweep France for the American struggle against the cruel tyranny of England actually began among the privileged classes of France.

Louis XVI, less skilled in detecting dangerous thoughts than his predecessors, saw no harm in Rousseau. His foreign minister, the Comte de Vergennes, was the sort of man to dismiss Rousseau's back-to-nature philosophy as sentimentality. He was playing a difficult role, trying to preserve France's right as a neutral nation to allow American ships to enter French ports, and at the same time attempting to lull the growing British suspicion that he was not on their side.

This was the state of affairs in France in the spring of 1776, when an ardent commoner, Caron de Beaumarchais, decided that France must do more than sit back and watch what was happening in America.

15

Pierre Augustin Caron de Beaumarchais

Beaumarchais

I know very well that to live is to fight and I would be perhaps desolate if I did not feel the contrary—that to fight is to live.

*B*eaumarchais is best known today as an author. The two delightful operas, *Barber of Seville* and *The Marriage of Figaro,* with music by Rossini and Mozart, respectively, are based on plays which Beaumarchais wrote. Figaro, the leading character of both, is valet to a Spanish count and in wit, intelligence, and moral standards far the superior of his titled employer.

"I have had to exert more knowledge and skill merely to survive than has been spent in a hundred years of governing the Spanish Empire," Figaro says at one point. And again: "I make haste to laugh at everything for fear of being obliged to weep at it." Alternately fortune smiles and frowns on Figaro. He is constantly in and out of trouble. Beaumarchais is said to have modeled Figaro on himself.

He was born Pierre-Augustin Caron in Paris on January 24, 1732. (Louis XV was then king of France; Louis XVI would not be born for another twenty-two years.) Monsieur Caron, his father, was a watchmaker with a small shop on the Rue Saint-Denis. Very young, Pierre started as an apprentice in his father's shop. At home, the entire family, both his parents and his five sisters, were musical and held concerts. Pierre mastered the guitar, the viola, the flute, and the harp.

In his teens Pierre once took up with some doubtful companions and sold watches and other things from the shop to pay for dinners and trips to the country. When his father found out, he sent his son away. Months later there was a reconciliation. Monsieur Caron wrote Pierre that he could come home if he would work from six in the morning until seven at night and adhere to other strict conditions. Weary of his exile, Pierre replied: "Monsieur and very dear and honored father . . . I sign your conditions in the firm determination to execute them with God's help."

He kept to his agreement, worked diligently, studied books on watchmaking in his spare time. At twenty-one he invented a timekeeping mechanism for watches that was smaller and more accurate than those in use. The official watch-maker of Versailles, Monsieur Lepaute, came and admired this invention and then proceeded to take credit for it. Outraged, Pierre wrote letters of protest to all involved, with the result that the Academy of Science denounced Lepaute and gave Pierre proper credit. This was his first of many fights against injustice.

Louis XV heard of the incident and invited Pierre to Versailles to explain how his watch mechanism worked. To please the sovereign, he made a watch so small it fit in a ring for Madame de Pompadour, the king's favorite. More orders flowed in from the royal family and the nobility. Because Pierre was tall, handsome, clever, and charming, he made an excellent impression at court, especially among the women.

An elderly man named Franquet sold him his court position as Clerk Controller of the Royal Household. The duties involved, which he performed expertly, were to wear his sword and escort the waiters who carried the meat to the royal table. Since being a Clerk Controller had far more prestige than watchmaking, Pierre abandoned the latter. When Monsieur Franquet died he married the old man's young and attractive widow. She lived only a few months. He inherited nothing save the name "de Beaumarchais" which he adopted from the name of some property Monsieur Franquet had once owned. Henceforth he called himself Caron de Beaumarchais.

Louis XV had four daughters who lived a secluded lonely life at court. Beaumarchais was recommended to give them lessons on the harp. Sometimes he arranged small concerts for them and wrote sketches for the little theater. Beaumarchais's popularity with the princesses aroused the jealousy of certain young nobles who persuaded a swordsman to challenge the handsome Clerk Controller to a duel. Beaumarchais wounded his opponent mortally, then, although he had time to escape, stayed to bind up his wounds. Saying only that he had got what he deserved, the dying swordsman gallantly refused even to name his opponent.

A rich banker, Monsieur Pâris-Duverney, sought Beaumarchais's acquaintance, for through him he hoped to gain access to the king. Monsieur Pâris-Duverney appreciated Beaumarchais's quick mind, taught him secrets of high finance, and bought him several lucrative posts, including that of Lieutenant General of Hunting. In this latter capacity, Beaumarchais acted as judge in charge of enforcing hunting laws in the king's hunting preserves. From his earnings he bought a large house and brought his family to live with him.

In 1764, at thirty-two, he spent a year in Spain to take care of some financial matters for Pâris-Duverney and to seek justice for his sister Lisette, whose young man Clavijo had broken his promise to marry her. He never did get Lisette and Clavijo together again, but he was very popular in the rather dull Spanish court and made some good friends. One of them was a liberal-minded young English diplomat, Lord Rochmont.

On his return he produced two plays, *Eugénie* and *The Two Friends,* and began working on a third, *The Barber of Seville.* He married a second time, and a year later became the father of a son.

In 1770, his rosy world began to fall apart. He lost his wife and soon afterward his son. His enemies at court claimed that he had poisoned both his wives. Voltaire came to his rescue. "Beaumarchais is too droll to kill his wives," he said. Pâris-Duverney also died that year. One of his heirs, the Comte de la Blâche, started a lawsuit against Beaumarchais, saying he had forged Pâris-Duverney's signature on a note for 15,000 francs. While the suit dragged on, a mad nobleman assaulted Beaumarchais, out of jealousy over an actress. Since his assailant, though insane, was of noble birth, Beaumarchais, though innocent, was sent to prison, where he stayed three months.

The Comte de la Blâche took advantage of his imprisonment to press his case. When Beaumarchais was released, he was told that the only way to win in court was to bribe Madame Goezman, the wife of the judge who was to try him. In spite of the bribe, the judge found him guilty. His house was seized and his furniture sold to pay his debts. Penniless and disgraced, Beaumarchais took up his pen and wrote a series of pamphlets about what had happened, so eloquent and so entertaining they aroused the sympathy of all Paris. Public sentiment forced the case to be reopened. Both Judge Goezman and his wife were condemned for taking bribes. But the charge of forgery still hung over Beaumarchais and because of this charge he had lost his civil rights.

At this low point in his fortunes, Louis XV sent for him to carry out a secret mission. A scandal writer living in London was about to publish a scurrilous attack on a highly placed court lady. Beaumarchais was entrusted with funds to pay him off and stop the book. His mission completed, he returned, hoping to receive a royal pardon. It was the luck of Figaro. He reached Paris in May of 1774, just as Louis XV lay dying of smallpox.

A few months later, another writer, also stationed in London, decided to prepare a vicious slander on Queen Marie Antoinette. Young Louis XVI, who had heard of Beaumarchais's success with the first blackmailer, sent him back to England. Again, Beaumarchais stopped the publication. As a reward, the king gave royal permission for the production of *The Barber of Seville,* which had previously been denied because of the play's gibes against nobility. It was an immediate success.

In the spring of 1775, about the time of the Battle of Concord in America, Louis XVI sent Beaumarchais for his third visit to London. This time his mission was to gather information on the English political scene. The assignment delighted him. He loved politics to madness, he said.

In London he saw Lord Rochmont, whom he had known in Spain, and through him met the controversial Mayor of London, John Wilkes, who was openly on the side of the American colonies and even advocated revolution within England. At a dinner given by Wilkes, Beaumarchais met his first American, a Virginia lawyer named Arthur Lee.

In his diplomatic reports to the king and Foreign Minister Comte de Vergennes, Beaumarchais added a colorful, and slightly exaggerated, account of how all America was up in arms against their British rulers. "All sensible people in England are convinced that the English colonies are lost to the mother country," he wrote Louis XVI on September 21, 1775, "and this is my opinion too."

American colonials rally to the cause of liberty.

20

A subsequent missive to his king shows a curiously aggressive tone for a man without civil rights: "Today when a violent crisis is advancing upon us with great strides, I am obliged to warn Your Majesty that the conservation of our American possessions [France's islands in the West Indies] and the peace which you so desire depends solely upon this one proposition—we must aid the Americans!"

When the king did not answer, he wrote to Vergennes, with a proposal to set up a dummy company through which supplies could be sent secretly to America.

Vergennes was already inclined to think that the advantage of humiliating England might outweigh the danger of encouraging a rebellion. Otherwise this cautious and conservative foreign minister would hardly have paid heed to a commoner, especially one known to have little respect for nobility. Incredible as it now seems, Vergennes went to the king with Beaumarchais's proposal. In April 1776, three months before the American Declaration of Independence, he wrote to Beaumarchais in England, authorizing the dummy company practically as Beaumarchais had suggested it:

Comte de Vergennes

It is necessary that in the eyes of the English government and of the Americans the operation should have essentially the aspect of an individual speculation. . . . We will secretly give you one million livres. We will try to obtain an equal sum from Spain. . . . With these two millions you will establish a big commercial house, and at your risk and peril you will supply the

The American Rattlesnake presenting Monsieur his Ally a Dish of Frogs.

British cartoons satirizing the French and American alliance.

Americans with arms, munitions, equipment, and all the other things that they will need to maintain the war. Our arsenal will deliver to you arms and munitions, but you will either replace them or pay for them. You will not demand money from the Americans, since they do not have any, but you will ask in return the produce of their soil which we will help you to sell in this country. . . .

He added that the "commercial house" must become self-supporting as soon as possible. The government funds would get it started, but Beaumarchais must depend on tobacco and rice from America to keep going. As a precaution, Vergennes had this letter copied by his son, whose handwriting could not be traced.

Beaumarchais was back in Paris in May. A new trial was held. He was cleared of all charges against him, and his civil rights were restored. Parisians carried him from the court on their shoulders, cheering and laughing.

As promised, Vergennes gave him a million livres from the French treasury. (Beaumarchais's receipt for it was found

Spirit of '76

after the French Revolution in secret government archives.) Spain, which also had grievances against England, contributed a second million two months later. Beaumarchais raised a third million from wealthy friends. As his headquarters he rented the former Dutch Embassy at No. 47 Rue Vieille du Temple. A discreet sign read: "Roderigue Hortalez & Company." Beaumarchais chose this romantic Spanish name for the new company, of which he, under the pseudonym of "Monsieur Durand" was the president.

The Ministry of War had recently changed its type of weapons, with the result that arsenals were crammed with war materials the army no longer needed. Beaumarchais was allowed to buy these up openly. Within a short time Hortalez & Company had 200 cannon, 25,000 guns, 30 brass mortars, and 200,000 pounds of gunpowder. The gunpowder was prepared according to a formula of French scientist Antoine Lavoisier, who had devised the best explosives then known. The guns were not only better than any the Americans had but were superior, according to some, to the Brown Bess carried by the British Redcoats.

Sometime in July, Beaumarchais received a visit from an American, referred to him by Vergennes, who introduced himself as Silas Deane of Connecticut. Deane posed as a private merchant but he had actually been sent by the Continental Congress to purchase military supplies in France. From then on he and Beaumarchais worked together in their common aim. Deane promised American ships to transport the supplies. When none appeared, Beaumarchais traveled to various French seaports to make arrangements with French shipowners. The essential thing was speed. News had reached Paris that the American army was practically destitute.

Lord Stormont, English Ambassador to France and head of a highly trained espionage system, learned that a fleet of heavily loaded transports were in the port of Le Havre and that Beaumarchais, under a pseudonym, was there too. Fuming, he went to Vergennes.

George Washington

"In the history of the world there is no such example of aid given rebels of a country with which one professes to be friendly," he said.

"We cannot stop smugglers," Vergennes told him calmly.

"Do smugglers go in fleets, sir?" Stormont demanded.

Vergennes was in a quandary. News from America was depressing. Following the colonists' bold Declaration of Independence on July 4, 1776, General William Howe had

23

occupied New York. General Washington had been defeated on Long Island and was retreating into New Jersey. With things going so badly, Vergennes knew he could not afford an open rift with England. He ordered Beaumarchais to detain his ships, but he closed his eyes when, soon afterward, Beaumarchais released them inconspicuously, one by one.

The first to sail was the *Amphitrite*. In flamboyant style, Beaumarchais wrote to Congress:

> Gentlemen:
> I believe that I ought to announce to you that the ship *Amphitrite*, of 400 tons, will sail with the first favorable wind for the first port of the United States that it can reach. The cargo of this ship, which is intended for you, consists of 4000 guns, 80 barrels of powder, 8000 pairs of shoes, and 3000 blankets; besides some officers of engineers and artillery; item, one German baron, formerly aide-de-camp to Prince Henry of Prussia; I think you can make a general of him, and am your servant,
>
> C. D. BEAUMARCHAIS.

The flippant way he spoke of "item, one German baron," shocked some of the more conservative members of Congress. The baron was Friedrich Wilhelm von Steuben, who had served under Frederick the Great of Prussia in the Seven Years' War. He was an excellent drillmaster and, as it turned out, an invaluable gift to America.

Baron von Steuben drilling Washington's army at Valley Forge.

Another Beaumarchais ship, the *Mercure,* which left from Nantes, docked at Portsmouth, New Hampshire, on April 30, 1777, bringing more arms, gunflints, and barrels of Lavoisier's excellent gunpowder, as well as bales of cloth, caps, stockings, and shoes. It was "welcomed with great joy and excitement by the inhabitants, who turned out to meet it clapping their hands."

The outfitting of the cargo ships was an exceedingly expensive matter. Beaumarchais awaited eagerly the return of his ships, hoping for cargo to pay his mounting debts. But when the ships reached port they were empty. Nor did he even receive an acknowledgment from Congress. This was due to an unfortunate misunderstanding.

After the Declaration of Independence, Congress appointed Benjamin Franklin, Silas Deane, and Arthur Lee, whom Beaumarchais had met in London, to represent the new United States of America in Paris. Franklin knew that Beaumarchais and Deane were working together and did not interfere. But Arthur Lee, in whom Beaumarchais had confided his plan for aiding America when it was still in an embryo stage, wrote the Congress Secret Committee of Correspondence that all materials from Hortalez & Company were a gift of the French government.

When Beaumarchais requested cargo in payment, Congress was understandably bewildered. They wrote to Vergennes who replied that Hortalez & Company was simply a private enterprise, but Lee's letters continued to flow in, casting doubts and accusing Deane and Beaumarchais of using Hortalez to make a personal profit. Most historians now agree that Arthur Lee had a jealous and unstable character. He even wrote unpleasant things about the irreproachable Benjamin Franklin. Congress had no way of knowing the truth and both Beaumarchais and Deane suffered. Deane became embittered, but Beaumarchais refused to let his enthusiasm flag.

By September 1777 Hortalez had shipped five million livres' worth of cargo with nothing in return. Beaumarchais borrowed enough to buy an old warship from the Ministry of Marine, rechristened her the *Fier Roderigue* (Proud Roderick), armed her with 66 cannon, and loaded her with cargo. Her papers said she was going to the West Indies. Lord Stormont found out about her, scoffed at the ship's papers, and went wrathfully to Prime Minister Maurepas. The *Fier Roderigue* had her sailing canceled.

In October, British General John Burgoyne surrendered his troops to American General Horatio Gates at Saratoga,

INDÉPENDANCE DES ÉTATS-UNIS.

Le 4 Juillet 1776, les Treize Colonies Confédérées (connues depuis sous le nom d'États-Unis) sont déclarées, par le Congrès, libres et indépendantes. N. Gérard, porteur des pouvoirs de LOUIS XVI, Roi de France, Benjamin Franklin pour les États-Unis, signent à Paris, le 6 Février 1777, un Traité d'amitié et de commerce, et un Traité d'alliance éventuelle, mis en vigueur par la déclaration de guerre survenue entre la France et l'Angleterre.

Le Comte d'Estaing, le Marquis de la Fayette, le Comte de Rochambeau, &c. combattent pour la cause des Américains, soutenue avec tant de gloire par le Général Washington. Capitulation faite le 19 Octobre 1782 par le Lord Cornwalis, dont le

désastre accélère la Paix. L'indépendance des États-Unis est reconnue par les Traités de Paix. Pénétrés de reconnaissance pour les services que LOUIS XVI leur a rendus, les États-Unis ont depuis fait élever à Philadelphie un monument qui en éternisera le souvenir. Cet exemple est d'autant plus mémorable, que les Siècles passés n'offrent aucun exemple de monumens élevés par des Républiques à la gloire d'un Souverain. Les Traités de Paix ont rendu aux Nations la liberté des mers; bienfait dont l'Europe est redevable à la générosité de LOUIS XVI. Le Port de Cherbourg, ouvrage immortel du règne de ce grand Prince, doit affermir cette liberté si utile aux Peuples.

A Paris chez Blin, Imprimeur en Taille-Douce, Place Maubert, N.º 17, vis à vis la rue des 3 Portes. A.P.D.R.

The Declaration of Independence as seen by a French artist.

New York. Beaumarchais was visiting Franklin at Passy two months later when a messenger from Boston arrived with the news. At once Beaumarchais leaped into his carriage and drove off at great speed so as to be the first to spread the word in Paris. His carriage overturned. "My right arm is cut," he wrote Vergennes, "the bones of my neck were nearly crushed . . . but the charming news from America is a balm to my wounds."

The victory at Saratoga provided the first concrete evidence that the Americans had a chance of winning their war. Beaumarchais besieged Vergennes with memoranda, urging that France openly join America. He was not the only one to do so, and Benjamin Franklin certainly deserved principal credit for the signing of the Franco-American treaty on February 6, 1778, by the terms of which France became an open ally of the new United States. But that treaty might

never have been made without the victory of Saratoga, won with guns and ammunition from Hortalez.

The month after the treaty, the *Fier Roderigue* set sail without interference, escorting a convoy of ten merchant ships, loaded with more supplies for the United States. Stormont could not stop it, but once more Beaumarchais was plagued by the bad luck which seemed always to follow his triumphs. Off the coast of the West Indies island of Grenada, his ships encountered a fleet under Admiral Comte d'Estaing, France's first navy support to America. D'Estaing con-scripted the *Fier Roderigue* into his own fleet, as he had the right to do.

The *Fier Roderigue* performed nobly in a subsequent battle with the English, but her captain was killed and she was riddled with shot. The king sent Beaumarchais a graceful letter of thanks for her services and an indemnity of two mil-lion livres, payable in installments. It was small consolation. Without their battleship to protect them, Beaumarchais's ten heavily ladened merchant ships were all captured or sunk.

Hortalez & Company managed to stay in business in 1783, thanks to Beaumarchais's energy and business acumen. Though Congress later recognized the country's debt to him and voted to reimburse him, in his lifetime Beaumarchais received nothing. He took the loss philosophically, as his creation, Figaro, took his misfortunes.

General John Burgoyne surrenders to General Horatio Gates.

Le Marquis de Lafayette

Lafayette

> I read, I study, I examine, I listen, I think, and out of all
> that I try to form an idea into which I put as much common
> sense as I can.

*I*n his school days Lafayette was assigned to write a
Latin essay on "The Superiority of the Spirit of Man to
Brute Force, Exemplified by Horse and Rider." Instead, he
described how a proud steed threw his rider and raced to
freedom. In later years, it seemed to him he had been writing
about the revolt of the Americans against British tyranny.

Baptismal records show his full name as Marie Joseph Paul
Yves Roch Gilbert du Motier, Marquis de Lafayette, Baron
de Vissac, Seigneur de St. Romain. He never suffered from
tyranny himself. The Château de Chavaniac in the province
of Auvergne in southern France, where he was born on
September 6, 1757, was part of a vast feudal estate. Before
he was two years old, his father was killed at the battle of
Minden in the War of Austrian Succession. His pretty
mother spent most of her time at Versailles. Lafayette,
brought up by an aged grandmother and an aunt, roamed
the forests looking for the legendary werewolf and made
friends with the peasants on the estate.

When he was eleven his mother enrolled him in the College
of Plessis in Paris. In this school for young aristocrats boys
dressed like their elders in embroidered coats, silk stockings,
and powdered hair. Compared to his proper schoolmates,
young Lafayette was something of a savage.

His mother and grandfather both died in 1770. At thirteen,
Lafayette inherited enormous properties in Auvergne, Brittany, and Touraine, profitably managed by trustees and law-
yers. As an orphan, a millionaire, and a marquis, he was
considered a worthy prospective son-in-law by the great lord,
the Duc d'Ayen-Noailles. Lafayette and the duke's second
daughter, Adrienne, were married in the spring of 1774, when
he was seventeen and she was fourteen. Though the marriage of these young people was arranged by their elders,
they developed a tender and lasting love.

Lafayette's influential father-in-law arranged for him to
take riding lessons with Louis XVI's youngest brother, the

*Gilbert and Adrienne de
Lafayette at the time of
their marriage.*

Count of Artois. As soon as he was eighteen, his father-in-law had him named an army captain. Early in 1775 he joined his garrison at Metz, in northeast France. The officer in command at Metz, the Comte de Broglie, had learned about the rebellion in America and had applied to Foreign Minister Vergennes to grant leave to certain qualified officers to go serve there. America, in his opinion, was an excellent fighting ground where the French could get revenge on the British. He even wanted to go himself, and replace General Washington, an ambition that was never realized.

In the next months Lafayette heard a good deal about America. His fellow officers could talk of little else. Life was dull with France at peace. They yearned to do glorious deeds overseas.

In December, Lafayette returned to Paris in time for the birth of his first daughter, Henriette. He dutifully presented himself at Versailles, but did not enjoy himself. Marie Antoinette made fun of his awkward dancing. He could not compete with the witty repartee of the courtiers. When he returned to Metz, he begged the Comte de Broglie for permission to go to America.

De Broglie sent him to Silas Deane, who tried to discourage him, saying he was too young. In desperation, Lafayette mentioned his high position in French society. His departure would create a sensation, he argued. This would inevitably react in America's favor. Deane yielded and gave him a contract as an American major general. He had no authority to grant such contracts but he thought he did.

When Lafayette failed to get passage on one of Beaumarchais's ships, he bought the *Victoire*. Wide-beamed and clumsy but seaworthy, the boat was at Bordeaux ready to sail by mid-March of 1777. Lafayette invited fourteen young officer friends and one older officer, Baron Johann de Kalb, to go along as his guests. Like Baron von Steuben, de Kalb was from Prussia. The son of a peasant, de Kalb had fled home at sixteen to avoid conscription, worked as a waiter in an Alsatian inn for a while, saved money, and become a French officer by forging a title of nobility. Louis XV had sent him to America back in 1768 as a spy; now he was returning to give his life for the American cause.

At the last moment, a royal courier brought Lafayette an order from Louis XVI forbidding him to leave. Lafayette convinced himself that his king was making a gesture to appease Lord Stormont, and the *Victoire* proceeded on her course. She reached North Inlet, about fifty miles from

Charleston, South Carolina, on June 13. A plantation owner entertained the officers overnight and lent them horses to proceed toward Philadelphia. De Kalb served as their interpreter at first. Later Lafayette learned to speak and write English, though his spelling was always atrocious.

His first impressions of America were exuberant. "What pleases me most is that all citizens are brothers," he wrote Adrienne. In Charleston, he visited the fort at Sullivan's Island, where General William Moultrie lined up his troops for inspection. Shocked, Lafayette noted that most were barefoot and that some had neither coats nor hats. Before he left he gave Moultrie money to buy clothing and arms for a hundred men.

In Philadelphia, on July 27, the French officers reported to Congress at Independence Hall, eager to be assigned to duty. After a long wait, a Congressman came out and told them coldly that America did not need any more officers; they had plenty of their own. Lafayette and his friends received this rebuff in stunned silence.

The truth was that Congress had been hounded by French officers claiming experience they did not have and demanding large salaries and high army rank. The West Indies colonial government of France had been using America as a dumping ground for incompetent officers they sought to get rid of. There had already been some unfortunate incidents with these officers; Congress had decided to call a halt.

That evening, in his room at the inn, Lafayette composed a letter begging Congress to allow him to serve without pay.

Independence Hall,
Philadelphia

31

None of his predecessors had used those words, "without pay." Congress was sufficiently impressed that they confirmed his contract with Deane, as a major general. De Kalb, a veteran of many wars, had his contract confirmed too. The only others accepted were Captain du Chosnoy, an engineer, and two members of Lafayette's personal staff, Major de Gimat and De la Colombe. Congress was firm in advising the rest to return to France.

On August 1, Lafayette was invited to dinner at City Tavern to meet George Washington. He wrote that he recognized him at once by "the majesty of his countenance and his tall form." Washington invited him to a review of his troops, as poorly clad as those on Sullivan's Island.

"We are rather embarrassed to show ourselves to an officer who has just left the army of France," Washington said apologetically.

"I am here, sir, to learn and not to teach," Lafayette told him.

At Washington's invitation, he stayed at the general's headquarters in Bucks County as an unofficial staff member. In view of his inexperience and poor English, he was not given an independent command. Washington made Lafayette happy by telling him that he considered himself to be his "father and friend." American officers were astounded, and a little jealous, at the growing attachment of their dignified and aloof general for this red-haired, blue-eyed French youth. As for Lafayette, he quite literally worshiped Washington.

Lafayette's affidavit of allegiance to the United States of America.

In August, General William Howe landed at Chesapeake Bay and began to march northward toward Philadelphia. With sprigs of green in their caps, the Continental Army marched down to drive them off. Lafayette rode happily at Washington's side. At Brandywine Creek, on September 11, the British attacked their rearguard troops. Washington sent Lafayette back to help out. He showed coolness and bravery in this, his first action under fire, but neither he nor anyone else could stem the rout. He did not know he was wounded—in the calf of his leg—until someone told him blood was dripping to the ground.

City Tavern, Philadelphia

The British occupied Philadelphia on September 26. Lafayette was convalescing at Bethlehem, Pennsylvania, in the home of a farmer. Washington's personal surgeon attended him. To Adrienne he wrote, "Messieurs the English paid me the compliment of wounding me slightly in the leg." The victory at Saratoga was some consolation for the loss of Philadelphia. From Adrienne came word of the birth of a second daughter, Anastasie, but she did not tell him that Henriette, their first daughter, had died.

Lafayette was still limping when he reported back to duty. By December he had sufficiently proved himself for Washington to give him command of a division. He looked after his men conscientiously and spent his own money to provide for them. The Board of War, acting without consultation with Washington, sent him to Albany, New York,

General Washington with General Nathanael Greene and Lafayette

General Washington and Lafayette visiting the troops at Valley Forge.

to head an expedition to attack Canada. This proved a futile undertaking, for when Lafayette arrived he found he had only half the promised troops and no supplies of food, clothing, sleighs, or ammunition. Disgusted, he wrote the Board of War for a new assignment. While waiting, he returned to share the hardships of Valley Forge with Washington, and to watch how General von Steuben, Beaumarchais's "gift" to Congress, was forging hungry, ragged troops into trained disciplined fighters.

News of the Franco-American treaty of alliance, signed in Paris on February 6, 1778, reached the colonies in May. Lafayette bounded into Washington's room at Valley Forge and kissed the general on both cheeks. He was wild with delight.

On orders from London, Sir Henry Clinton, who had replaced General William Howe as commander of the British forces in North America, evacuated Philadelphia and began a long march toward New York. The Continental Army encountered them at Monmouth on June 28. Washington's presence of mind saved them from a shameful retreat. "I thought then, as now, that never had I beheld so superb a man," Lafayette wrote later. He himself fought until, smoke-blackened, he sank exhausted under an apple tree. When he awakened he found that General Washington had spread his own cloak over him (so legend has it).

The first French fleet sent to America's aid following the alliance arrived the following month, under Admiral d'Estaing, the same who had commandeered the *Fier*

34

Roderigue. A combined French-American operation to oust the British from Rhode Island was planned, but through no fault of d'Estaing's it ended in failure and the French fleet left for the West Indies. For Lafayette, it was a personal defeat.

At his request, Washington granted him a leave of absence to return to France. Congress gave him a vote of thanks for his services. "He is the idol of Congress, of the army, and the people of America," wrote the French Ambassador at Philadelphia to Vergennes. Lafayette's farewell to Washington was "very tender and very painful." He reached Brest on February 6, 1779, after a fast crossing of twenty-six days.

For having gone to America against the king's orders, he was sentenced to the light punishment of a week's house arrest. This gave him a chance to make up to Adrienne for the pain his absence had caused her and to get acquainted with little Anastasie. Then he was off to Versailles to file a report and ask the king's pardon.

His success was tremendous. Marie Antoinette opened the court ball with this "hero of two worlds." Young nobles listened enviously to his tales. Through the queen's influence, this American major general was made a French colonel and granted the privilege of paying 80,000 francs for

Lafayette reports to Louis XVI and Marie Antoinette.

35

George Washington, from a painting by John Trumbull.

a regiment. His friends were incredulous when he told them that in America no one bought regiments and that men were promoted on merit alone.

America had changed him. Words like "liberty" and "equality" meant something to him now. America, America, America rang in his heart day and night. He made the rounds of the king's ministers with a series of suggestions for aiding their ally, mostly impractical. One of them—to take 2000 men to sea on vessels commanded by the American sea captain John Paul Jones, capture English port cities and demand ransom of them—captured the fancy of both Jones and Benjamin Franklin, but was vetoed by the French government.

In the summer of 1779, Lafayette was ordered to report to Le Havre, on the English channel. Unknown to him, a plan for a large-scale invasion of England by France and Spain was in the offing. (Spain had formed an alliance with France against England in April.) As Quartermaster Inspector General, Lafayette worked hard and fervently. But the Spanish fleet was late in arriving, a smallpox epidemic spread on the French ships, and to Lafayette's great disappointment the invasion was abandoned. He was back in Paris on Christmas Eve when Adrienne gave birth to a son. The proud father named him Georges Washington Lafayette and sent off a letter to his American commander in chief about his namesake.

The following January of 1780 he was informed that the king was sending a large expeditionary force to America. The command was given not to Lafayette, though he yearned for it, but to Lieutenant General Rochambeau, a veteran with nearly forty years of military experience. Lafayette dashed off to give Rochambeau the benefit of his American experience. The Americans were in need of everything, he told him. He must take flints for muskets, harness for the horses, flour, bricks for ovens, as well as needles, thread, shoe leather, tools, and beads for the Indians. Courteously, Rochambeau promised to neglect nothing.

Lafayette's own assignment was to go ahead on a fast frigate and tell Washington the expedition was coming. He reached Washington's headquarters in Morristown, New Jersey, on May 10. Washington received the news with pleasure, though he had reason to be skeptical of French aid. The previous September, Admiral d'Estaing had returned to try to help the Americans recapture Savannah, Georgia. The allies had been repulsed with severe losses—a second defeat on top of that at Rhode Island, and not as yet any compensating victories.

The war picture was gloomy. New York was still in British hands and New York harbor was filled with British ships. It was getting harder for Congress to find funds to support this five-year-old war. Continental paper currency had so depreciated that a captain's full month's pay would scarcely buy a pair of shoes. Two days after Lafayette's arrival, General Benjamin Lincoln surrendered Charleston to Sir Henry Clinton. It was evident to Lafayette that only Washington's dogged determination held his ill-clad, ill-fed, unpaid army together.

When Rochambeau landed in Newport on July 12, with 5500 men and a fleet of eight battleships, Washington sent Lafayette to convey his greetings. Rochambeau seemed disappointed the American general could not have come in person, since there was so much to discuss. Lafayette, feeling he was speaking for his beloved Washington, explained to Rochambeau in great detail how vital it was to liberate New York at once. Having built up his hopes so high, he found it well-nigh impossible to accept Rochambeau's veto to his plan on the grounds that the British, with their large fleet firmly ensconced in New York harbor, had naval superiority.

For once, Lafayette's enthusiasm and impatience outweighed his military judgment. He continued to press Rochambeau to attack New York until he saw that the general was getting annoyed with him.

In September, at their first meeting held in Hartford, Connecticut, Washington and Rochambeau discussed the same subject. Lafayette was interpreter. The outcome was that Washington agreed that it would be impractical to try to take New York until the reinforcements Rochambeau expected had arrived. Much as it pained him, Lafayette had to resign himself to their decision.

Benedict Arnold

In February 1781, Washington gave Lafayette his most important assignment to date, to take 1200 troops and reinforce General von Steuben in Virginia. General Benedict Arnold, who had betrayed the Americans and gone over to the British, was now in that state, leading British troops on inland forays to burn and loot and terrorize the countryside. Lafayette was delighted to have a chance to avenge his adopted country against a man whose very name had become a symbol of treachery.

The problems that faced Lafayette were multiple. His troops, New Englanders and New Jerseymen, feared the heat

and malaria of the south, and some deserted. Lafayette called them together. He was going to face the British, he told them, but if any of them were afraid they should step out of the ranks and he would give them a pass to go home. Not one man stepped forth.

It was up to Lafayette, in this war run on a shoestring, to see that his men were clothed and fed and to arrange transport for supplies. In Philadelphia, he hounded Congress until he got a month's back pay for the troops. At a later date, in Baltimore, Maryland, he borrowed 2000 guineas against a draft on his French agent to buy them overalls, hats, shoes, and cloth for shirts, and persuaded the women of the town to make the shirts. To get to Richmond, Virginia, more quickly, he arranged to have half of his men ride in wagons while the others walked; then he switched them around so the tired could rest. One officer said the system imparted "an air of novelty and frolic" to their journey. In Virginia, he refused to pull rank on von Steuben, though he had been the first to be commissioned major general and thus outranked him.

The original plan was to bottle up Benedict Arnold at Portsmouth and to have part of the French fleet at Newport come and cut off reinforcements from the sea. But spies found out about the movements of the French ships and English ships drove them back. To relieve Arnold, General Clinton sent General William Phillips, who had commanded the artillery at the Battle of Minden where Lafayette's father was killed. Lafayette did not get the chance to take revenge against either him or the traitor. Arnold was recalled and Phillips died of fever on May 15. The British command was taken over by Lord Charles Cornwallis, the most brilliant general in the British Army.

General Anthony Wayne and his 800 Pennsylvania troops joined Lafayette on June 10. Their total forces still numbered only about 3000, compared to over 7000 under Cornwallis. "Were I to fight a battle I should be cut to pieces," Lafayette wrote Washington. "Were I to decline fighting, the country would think itself given up. I am therefore determined to skirmish."

All during June and July, Lafayette harassed Cornwallis without exposing his own men. On July 6, at Green Spring near Jamestown, Virginia, Cornwallis nearly trapped Wayne's Pennsylvanians, but otherwise there were no major encounters. To Lafayette's private bewilderment, Cornwallis retreated as he advanced. By August the British had moved

General Anthony Wayne

Statue of George Washington in Richmond, Virginia.

down to Yorktown, on a peninsula in Chesapeake Bay bounded by the James and York rivers. There they began to build defensive fortifications.

To block Cornwallis from the mainland, Lafayette set up headquarters near Williamsburg, Virginia, about twelve miles up the peninsula. He let his men rest and caught up with his neglected correspondence: "When one is twenty-three, has an army to command and Lord Cornwallis to oppose, the time that is left is none too long for sleep."

In truth, throughout this long and frustrating campaign, Lafayette showed a maturity, tact, and wisdom utterly astounding for a youth of twenty-three. Several American officers had resented that Washington should entrust this command to a foreigner. Lafayette was resolved to justify his general's faith in him, and he succeeded beyond expectation.

From his headquarters, Washington kept him informed of new developments. Rochambeau and his troops had joined Washington in Lafayette's absence. They had been awaiting the arrival of a certain Admiral de Grasse with a fleet from the West Indies to launch the long-postponed attack on New York. Then, in the latter part of August, the French engineer General du Portail in person brought Lafayette a dispatch from Washington announcing a change in plans. He and Rochambeau were bringing their armies south to the Chesapeake. Admiral de Grasse was sailing there, not to New York. Keep Cornwallis bottled up, Washington urged him.

The French fleet appeared on the horizon on August 30. Lafayette sent emissaries out to welcome them. The admiral had brought along 3000 French infantrymen from the West Indies, under the command of the Marquis de Saint-Simon. Graciously, the Marquis volunteered to put himself and his men under Lafayette's command, and proposed an immediate assault on Cornwallis' defenses. Lafayette refused this tempting offer. Rochambeau and Washington were not far away now. He did not wish to deprive either of them of their share of the glory that suddenly seemed so certain.

*Benjamin Franklin assuming his place among the great of all times,
as depicted by a French artist.*

Benjamin Franklin

All Europe is on our side of the question; as far as applause and good wishes can carry them. . . . 'Tis a common observation here, that our cause is *the cause of all mankind,* and that we are fighting for their liberty in defending our own.

No American loved and appreciated France as did Benjamin Franklin. No American was more loved by the French people than he. Though he never faltered in his allegiance to his native land, he felt at home in France; France became his adopted country. While Lafayette and the French volunteers were shedding blood on American soil, Franklin was carrying on a singlehanded diplomatic battle in Paris and Versailles. He sought to forge bonds that would link the French nation irretrievably to the American cause, and his success was phenomenal.

This son of a Boston candlemaker was born in 1706, one of a large family of seventeen children. Their father could not provide luxuries for them, sometimes not even necessities, but he invited men of learning to dinner to improve their minds. At twelve, young Benjamin was apprenticed to his older brother, James, a printer. Benjamin read widely and wrote articles for his brother's newspaper under the pseudonym of "Mrs. Silence Dogood." Once he had Mrs. Dogood quote from the London *Journal:* "Without Freedom of Thought, there can be no such Thing as Wisdom; and no such Thing as public liberty without Freedom of Speech." When he was seventeen he had a quarrel with James, who was sometimes harsh with him, and ran away.

Young Benjamin Franklin arrived in Philadelphia like a vagabond, in rumpled clothes and pockets bulging with spare socks and shirts. Within twenty-four hours he had found a job with a Philadelphia printer. Five years later he opened his own printing shop. By that time he had married Deborah, who did not share his many interests but remained a loyal wife as long as she lived. In 1732 he began publication of *Poor Richard's Almanack,* which outsold all other almanacs because homely wisdom and terse maxims were included with information on weather and the planting of crops.

By 1736 he had six printers working under him, and expanded his activities. He served as clerk to the Pennsylvania

Franklin's birthplace

Assembly, and as Philadelphia postmaster. He invented the Franklin stove, which heated rooms evenly and gave off no smoke. He organized the American Philosophical Society, the first scientific organization in the colonies. He promoted Philadelphia's first paid police force and America's first fire department.

At forty-two he was a rich man by contemporary standards and decided to retire. He then began making experiments with electricity, including his most celebrated one of flying a kite with a key attached to the end of the string during a thunderstorm. Curious about everything, he explored other scientific fields as well. After he invented the lightning rod, the London Royal Society made him its first American member.

In 1757 he went to England as the official representative of Pennsylvania colony. Deborah, who was afraid of the sea, would not go with him and died in his absence. For most of the next seventeen years he stayed in England, always promoting the interests of the colonies. His friends there included simple people, famous scientists, and great lords and ladies. Foreign ambassadors living in London treated him as their equal and, toward the end of his stay, as their teacher.

His first visit to France was in August 1767, on a summer vacation. Until that time he had shared some of the American prejudices against their enemy of the French and Indian War, but hardly had his boat docked at Calais when the charm of the country began to work its magic. Even the porters, he noted, were more polite than English porters. Still it shocked him to learn that the excellent road to Paris, "paved with smooth stones . . . and rows of trees on each side," was maintained by peasants who worked on it two months a year without pay.

Franklin's experiments with electricity had made him world-famous, and French scientists welcomed him with open arms, assuring him they were *Franklinists,* a word they had invented. He visited Versailles and was overwhelmed with "the number of statues, figures, urns, &c., in marble and bronze of exquisite workmanship." He met Louis XV, "who did me the honor of taking some notice of me."

Franklin made a second trip to France two years later, in 1769. On both voyages he made French friends, with whom he corresponded over the next years. In the meantime, unrest was increasing in America. In his capacity as agent from Massachusetts, from 1770 on, he did all in his power to persuade the British Parliament to pursue a more tolerant course. In the spring of 1774, when he realized his efforts were useless, he returned to America. He was on the high seas at the time of Battle of Concord on April 19, when the war started.

Two days after he reached home, he was chosen as Pennsylvania delegate to the Second Continental Congress. That September he helped form the Secret Committee of Congress, the aim of which was to purchase war supplies from foreign countries. It was this committee which sent Silas Deane to Paris, where he fortunately met Beaumarchais and Hortalez & Company. Franklin also served on the Committee of Secret Correspondence, created to establish closer relations with foreign nations.

Far longer than some members of Congress, he kept hoping for reconciliation with England. "We have not yet applied to any power for assistance," he wrote the British scientist and American sympathizer, Joseph Priestley, in July 1775. "Perhaps we never may; yet it is natural to think of it, if we are pressed." Six months later, he was approached by a mysterious "Monsieur Achard de Bonvouloir," who, though posing as an Antwerp merchant, was actually a French officer sent by Foreign Minister Vergennes. Bonvouloir confided that France was willing to let American ships come into French ports to pick up cargoes, but only if they could be certain America intended to declare independence from England.

Of course America was going to declare independence, Franklin assured Bonvouloir blandly. Six months later came the Declaration of Independence. Franklin was on the committee charged with the responsibility of preparing it.

In September 1776, Congress unanimously, and in great secrecy, elected to send him to France to head a commission of three—himself, Silas Deane, and Arthur Lee. Their real mission was to present the American cause to the French government and to seek aid. Ostensibly, Franklin was traveling as a private citizen. He set sail on October 27 on the sloop *Reprisal.* With him were his two grandsons, Temple Franklin, who was eighteen, and Benjamin Franklin Bache, age seven. The *Reprisal* landed at the small port town of Auray on December 4, and Franklin went on by carriage to Nantes.

A group of prominent Nantes citizens were waiting to greet the celebrated American. They were astounded. Instead of a curled and powdered wig, a fox fur cap covered his thin gray straight hair. He wore a plain brown homespun suit with white stockings and buckled shoes, and had spectacles on his nose because, at seventy, vanity was not so important as seeing clearly. He carried a plain crabtree cane.

"A *primitive!*" people exclaimed delightedly. By the next day the women of Nantes had devised a hair-do *à la Franklin,* with their hair piled high in a curly mass to imitate his fur cap. Balls and dinners were held in his honor.

His reception at Nantes was but a prelude to Paris, where his printer, Barbour Debourg, had for several days been distributing circulars announcing his arrival. Crowds followed him everywhere. Since his last visit his reputation had spread. *Le Bonhomme Richard,* as the French translated the maxims of Poor Richard, had gone through three editions. It was read by the sophisticated nobles, and by coachmen, valets, and chambermaids. People thought of Franklin as a friend of mankind, and this at a time when mankind had very few friends among those highly placed. He was, for them, the personification of the "natural man," the man unspoiled by society, exactly as Rousseau had envisioned him. Franklin, who had spent years fending with British aristocrats, neither encouraged nor discouraged this belief.

In the country of Voltaire, Rousseau, and Montesquieu, he was accepted as one of the world's truly great. His benign manner, his humor, his unaffected manners, enchanted the common people, accustomed to the pomp and pompousness of French nobility.

No crowds gathered around his two fellow commissioners, Silas Deane and Arthur Lee. Deane accepted this with good grace and made himself useful where he could. Arthur Lee, the jealous one, reacted unpleasantly, but his numerous sly thrusts evoked only one placid rebuke from Franklin.

For all his modest airs, Franklin was a wily diplomat. Three weeks after his arrival, he and Deane were received at Versailles by Foreign Minister Vergennes. Though Deane dressed up for the occasion, Franklin appeared, without a wig, in his usual brown homespun suit. He presented the greetings of Congress. Vergennes assured him of the protection of France as long as he stayed. They exchanged a few more pleasantries, touched briefly on the situation in America, and that was all. But from then on Vergennes avoided dealing with any American except Benjamin Franklin.

The next night he attended a reception held by the Marquise du Deffand, an old woman, very rich and very pro-British. Her guests included some of the most important personages in Europe. It was taken for granted that Monsieur Franklin of Philadelphia would not be able to compete in this brilliant company. He was much too clever to try. All evening he sat quietly, listening attentively to what everyone had to say, even the ladies. The guests were amazed. Americans had the reputation of being bold and self-assertive. But this "Monsieur Franklin" they decided, was a sage, a patriarch! They could not praise him enough. After that the aristocracy joined the scientists and everyday Parisians in seeking his company.

A few days later, Louis XVI, urged on by Vergennes, authorized a secret loan of two million livres for the American cause, not connected with the Hortalez funds. Franklin had, without trickery or conniving, scored his first diplomatic victory. Wisely, he did not press for further meetings at Versailles but went about his own affairs.

During January 1777, he began attending meetings of the French Academy of Science. His illustrious colleagues inscribed his name in the minutes, an honor rarely given to

Benjamin Franklin is received with high honor at Versailles.

45

a foreigner. He became an avid sightseer and visited all the fine libraries and museums in Paris. His scholarly activities suited Vergennes perfectly. He informed British diplomats that Franklin's visit had no political significance and that he was in Paris only to renew old acquaintances. The whole course of Franklin's life, Vergennes said, was "candid and guileless."

Lord Stormont, English ambassador in France, remained skeptical. While Franklin was in England he had got the better of three successive English foreign ministers, Stormont told Vergennes. The good doctor was never so formidable as when he seemed to have no time for state affairs.

In March, Franklin moved from his Paris hotel to Passy in the suburbs. An ardent American partisan, Le Ray de Chaumont, turned over to him a charming mansion in the garden of his beautiful estate of Valentinois. Little Benjamin Bache went to boarding school, while Temple, Franklin's older grandson, acted as his secretary. Franklin kept his own servants and a carriage and a pair of horses. Even this modest outlay caused some repercussions in Congress, where certain members accused him of extravagance.

Unostentatiously, he began cultivating foreign ambassadors resident in Paris. He helped the Russian Ambassador out of a scrape, thus winning his enduring friendship. He was on excellent terms with the Spanish Minister. With foresight, Franklin already saw the United States as a world power, for which friendly relations with foreign nations would be a necessity. Solely by his unique personality, he won over practically the entire European continent. The growing unpopularity of England, largely traceable to Franklin's influence, was indicated in a wry speech which Lord Shelburne made to the British House of Peers. Their king, George III, he said, had but two enemies: "the whole world and his own Ministry."

In France, Franklin's personal popularity increased. His picture hung above the mantle in thousands of French homes. Snuffboxes were adorned with his image on enamel medallions, and tinier reproductions were set in rings. He appeared on watches, vases, handkerchiefs, and pocket knives. Sculptors made busts in marble, bronze, and plaster. To his daughter, Sally, Franklin wrote that her father's face was "as well known as that of the moon." It pleased him that the French did not call him a rebel, as did the English, but an insurgent.

He was given sole credit for writing the Declaration of Independence (which Thomas Jefferson drafted) and the

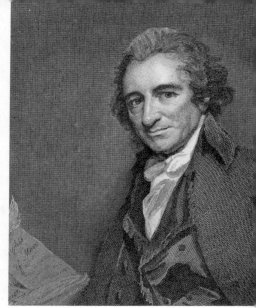

Thomas Jefferson   *Thomas Paine*

stirring pamphlet *Common Sense* (under the pseudonym of Thomas Paine), and for singlehandedly fomenting the American revolt, a claim to fame spread by the British.

Lord Stormont also started a rumor that Franklin was a deserter and had quarreled with Congress. Franklin ignored this personal attack, but he felt Stormont was going too far when he started saying that 4000 Americans had been lost in a certain battle and their general killed. "Truth is one thing, Stormont is another," he commented. In Parisian slang, the verb "to stormont" became a synonym for "to lie."

Titled French women were ecstatic when he accepted an invitation to dinner. At the country château of Madame d'Houdetot, his hostess met him at the gate, greeting him with verses of praise. Between courses at dinner, a count or a viscount rose and recited rhymed compliments. After coffee, his host spoke at length, comparing Franklin to the Swiss patriot William Tell, to Franklin's advantage. On his departure the guests escorted him to his coach, still reciting laudatory couplets.

More to Franklin's taste were evenings he spent with his neighbor, Madame Helvétius, the highly intelligent widow of a French scholar. At her salon he met the Encyclopedist Denis Diderot, Antoine Lavoisier, discoverer of oxygen and inventor of a highly explosive gunpowder, and the former French minister of finance, Baron de Turgot, who said of him, "He snatched the lightning from the sky and the scepter from the tyrants."

So many French officers begged him for commissions to serve in America that in jest he composed a form letter:

47

". . . As to this gentleman, I must refer you to himself for his character and merits, with which he is certainly better acquainted than I can possibly be. . . ." In a different vein he wrote to Washington about Lafayette: "He is exceedingly beloved, and everybody's good wishes attend him; we cannot but hope he may meet with such a reception as will make the country and his expedition agreeable to him."

Except for Washington's victory at Trenton in the Christmas of 1776, there was little hopeful news from America that first year. Franklin remained staunchly optimistic. When a visitor reported that General Howe had taken Philadelphia, Franklin countered, "I beg your pardon, sir. Philadelphia has taken Howe." A month later, while Beaumarchais was calling, a Boston messenger brought the more appetizing news of the victory at Saratoga—no mere skirmish but the capture of an entire British army. It was what Franklin had been waiting for.

With Deane and Lee, he drew up a formal proposal for an alliance with France and dispatched it to the foreign minister. Vergennes's reaction was sympathetic but cautious. Such an alliance could not be made without the consent of Spain, he said. The response from Spain came more than a month later and was negative. Temporarily, negotiations were at a standstill.

In the meantime England had sent an envoy named Paul Wentworth to discuss with Franklin terms for an armistice: a return to the colonial status before 1763 with high rewards in money, title, and position for those Americans who used their influence to achieve the armistice. Franklin was not interested. Nonetheless, after the impasse with Vergennes he invited Wentworth, Silas Deane, and his assistant, Edward Bancroft, to dinner.

As he anticipated, the little dinner party was promptly reported to Vergennes, who could only deduce that America was negotiating for peace. This would mean that England would emerge stronger than ever, once more a threat to the security of France. The following day Louis XVI's Council of Ministers voted unanimously to enter into an alliance with the United States. The treaty was signed on February 6, 1778, by Conrad-Alexandre Gérard of the French foreign office, and by Franklin, Arthur Lee, and Silas Deane.

On March 20, the three Americans were invited to Versailles to meet Louis XVI. The young king received them graciously. "Gentlemen, I would like you to assure Congress of my friendship," he said. Franklin, for once in his life, was overcome with emotion and wept. Later the American guests met Marie Antoinette in her gambling room. She made Franklin stand beside her while she placed her bets.

That September, Congress elected Franklin sole plenipotentiary to France. Thus he became America's first official ambassador in a foreign land. His embassy was a few rented rooms in Passy. His staff was his grandson Temple, who copied dispatches with a quill pen. Old and ill, suffering from gout and other ailments, Franklin was in effect consul general, consultant on American affairs, propaganda agent for America, and, in fact if not in name, overseas Secretary of the Navy. In this latter capacity, he commissioned privateers to disrupt English coastal traffic, which they did with great success. After the French rejected Lafayette's proposal to go with John Paul Jones to capture English port towns for

King Louis XVI received Benjamin Franklin on his first mission to France in March, 1778.

49

The Bonhomme Richard *captures the British frigate* Serapis.

ransom, Franklin persuaded the French government to turn over a 40-gun French frigate for Jones. Rechristened the *Bonhomme Richard,* it captured the far superior English frigate, the *Serapis,* in a notable sea battle.

Franklin's most unpleasant task was to keep the French government supplying America with money. This he performed admirably. With the king and Vergennes he was always calm, discreet, and frank. He listened attentively to their point of view, referred the matter to Congress, and then waited for the right moment to give them the views of Congress. Usually he got what he asked.

In the spring of 1781, Colonel John Laurens arrived in Paris, sent by Congress, who were in a financial crisis and needed additional funds. Franklin had anticipated the crisis and could inform Laurens that he already had a promise of an outright gift of six million livres from the French government.

Congress continued to send demands for more funds, but Franklin had to tell them that France's resources were limited. In truth, the costs of the American war had exhausted the royal treasury, and it was only by the shrewd manipulations of Finance Minister Jacques Necker that the huge deficit remained concealed as long as it did.

Had it not been for the diplomacy and quiet persistence of Benjamin Franklin, it is unlikely that Louis XVI and his

50

Hotel de Valentinois

Yard and gardens of the Hotel de Valentinois

ministers would have become so deeply involved in the American cause. "He possessed the confidence of that government (France) in the highest degree," wrote Thomas Jefferson later, "insomuch, that it may truly be said, that they were more under his influence, than he under theirs."

The British historian George Otto Trevelyan, who deplored the American rebellion and the folly of the British Parliament which led up to it, paid Franklin the biggest tribute of all. "He was a great ambassador," Trevelyan wrote, "of a type which the world has never seen before, and will never see again until it contains another Franklin."

Le Comte de Rochambeau

Rochambeau

I am the friend of their [America's] friends and the foe of
their foes.

J ean Baptiste Donatien de Vimeur, Comte de Rochambeau, was fifty-five years old and had thirty-nine years of
military experience behind him when he was given the assignment Lafayette so desired, as commander of the French expeditionary army to America. Rochambeau was born July
1, 1725, at Vendôme, 110 miles south-southwest of Paris.
His family had sent their oldest sons to battle since the time
of the Crusades. In spite of their huge château on the banks
of the river Loire, they were not rich.

As a second son, young Rochambeau began his studies for
the priesthood, but at fifteen, following the death of his older
brother, he was transferred to the Paris Academy for
Officers. A year later the War of the Austrian Succession
(1741–1748) broke out. Rochambeau joined the Régiment
Saint-Simon as a standard-bearer and served beyond the
Rhine. At eighteen he was promoted to captain. He became
a colonel at twenty-one after taking an enemy-held fortress
in The Netherlands on a precipice considered impregnable.
His family scraped up the funds to pay the king for his
regiment, as was the custom in the eighteenth-century French
army.

He was severely wounded at the battle of Lauffeld, when
he led his regiment against the center of the enemy's line.
In recognition, Louis XV invited him to ride in the royal
carriage and dine with his intimates. Rochambeau commented: "It would be difficult to give any adequate reason
for this elaborate etiquette."

In 1749, the year after peace was declared, he married
Jeanne-Thérèse d'Acosta, daughter of a rich Portuguese merchant. They spent their honeymoon at Vendôme in preference to Versailles. Their son, Donatien-Marie-Joseph de
Vimeur, was born in 1755. Rochambeau became a brigadier
general at the outbreak of the Seven Years' War in 1756—the
year before Lafayette was born.

His men were always the best-trained in the garrison. "The
bravery of your troops has not surprised me," wrote Lord

Granby, his enemy and the officer in charge of the British cavalry, "since learning from your officers of the great respect every one in the corps has for their general and for the confidence they so rightly place in his judgment." Though he demanded strict discipline, Rochambeau never forgot the words of an old marshal: "I don't tell you to try to deserve your men's respect; I tell you to try to deserve their love." "Papa Rochambeau," his soldiers called him affectionately.

To supplement regular troops, Rochambeau formed a corps of *chasseurs* (light infantry), men of slight build trained to move quickly. After the war, when thirty-three commoners who had received temporary commissions as officers were slated for discharge, he came strongly to their defense. He saw no reason why qualified officers should be discharged solely because they were not of noble birth. His most pungent criticism of the many campaigns in which he fought was that none of the generals thought in terms of long-range planning.

In 1779, the year after the Franco-American treaty, he was sent to Normandy to train troops for the proposed invasion of England. He probably met Lafayette at this time. When the invasion was called off, Rochambeau, who was suffering from old wounds and inflammatory rheumatism, received permission to retire. As his carriage was waiting in front of his Paris mansion to take him to Vendôme in January of 1780, a royal messenger arrived to summon him to Versailles. The king informed him he was slated to head the expeditionary

Rochambeau's expeditionary army embarked for America from the port of Brest.

force to America. He put aside his dream of returning to private life.

Preparations in the next months were intensive. Rochambeau saw young Lafayette, who bubbled over with advice as to what he should take and how he ought to treat the Americans. The older man was not too proud to accept useful suggestions from this youth who might well be a major general in the American army but was only a colonel at home. There was no lack of recruits. Soldiers were happy to serve under such a general as Rochambeau, and young officers used all their influence at court for permission to go along.

The fleet that assembled at Brest under the command of Admiral d'Arsac de Ternay had eight ships of the line (battleships), six frigates, three cutters, thirty-six transports, and one hospital ship. Rochambeau had hoped for more. These vessels could only take 5500 of the nearly 8000 officers and men gathered hopefully at Brest. Rochambeau promised those left behind that they could join him on the second expedition, which he firmly believed would follow.

Among the lucky officers were the handsome Vioménil brothers, one a baron, the other a count; the scholarly Chevalier de Chastellux, author of a book on public welfare praised by Benjamin Franklin; the Vicomte de Noailles, Lafayette's brother-in-law; the Marquis de Montesquieu, grandson of the great philosopher; the Swedish Comte Axel de Fersen, a favorite of Marie Antoinette; the Vicomte de Rochambeau, the general's twenty-five-year-old son; and the dashing Duc de Lauzun, whose departure caused many sighs from the Versailles court beauties. Lauzun was in command of the

55

Lauzun Legion, some two hundred brave and boisterous cavalrymen mostly of Polish or Irish birth. There were a score more high-ranking officers. Those who did not have regiments to command served as aides to Rochambeau and his generals. Most of them wrote memoirs or kept diaries about their American adventure.

At the last moment Comte Alexandre Berthier and his younger brother clung to the rope ladders, begging to be taken aboard as simple sailors. The gruff Admiral de Ternay told them he had no place "to stuff them." Undaunted, the two brothers sailed on the next frigate to cross the ocean and served with Rochambeau for the full campaign.

A German view of the landing of the French expeditionary army at Newport, Rhode Island.

The fleet set sail in May. To avoid a British fleet leaving about the same time the Admiral took a southern route. The journey lasted seventy days. About a third of the men fell ill with scurvy in their overcrowded quarters and there were a few deaths. It was Rochambeau's first sea voyage. He spent much of his time studying the stars and mastering the arts of navigation. Probably he reread the king's detailed and explicit instructions, which stressed that Rochambeau's troops must serve as an auxiliary to Washington's armies. Under no circumstances were the French to give the impression they were taking over the American war.

From an English brig captured off North Carolina, they learned that Charleston had surrendered to General Clinton. American pilots steered them from Martha's Vineyard to the harbor of Newport, which the British had evacuated the previous October. On July 11, 1780, they dropped anchor. Because of a heavy fog they could not see the standards with the French fleur-de-lis, which Washington had ordered raised for them along the coast.

The frigate *Hermione* took Rochambeau and his general staff to shore. "There was no one about in the streets," wrote Rochambeau, "only a few sad and frightened faces in the windows." He later learned that Tory sympathizers had been slandering them. Finally they found some leading citizens whom Rochambeau assured, with all the eloquence the occasion demanded, that his troops were but an advance guard of a far more powerful army and that they were going to stay as long as they were needed.

Within twenty-four hours flags were hung out and there were fireworks. General William Heath, a stout and bald farmer, arrived tardily to greet them in Washington's name. Heath arranged hospital care for the sick soldiers and sailors and offered the welcome service of his Rhode Island and Massachusetts militia to fortify their sites. "The great and small artillery landed by our generous allies . . . exceed anything of the kind ever seen here," reported the Newport *Mercury*.

Rochambeau sent off a long letter to General Washington. "I join to this letter a copy of my instructions," he concluded, "and even of my secret instructions also, as I do not choose to have any secrets from my general." Thus he set the tone for their relationship.

The townspeople were impressed with this stocky, good-tempered French general, who was not frivolous, as they imagined the French, nor haughty, as the English had been. Moreover he asked no favors and paid for everything he needed, even the campsite for his men. The discipline of his troops pleased everyone. They did not touch the apples on the heavily laden trees, and pigs and chickens wandered unharmed through their camps.

On July 22, British ships were sighted off Newport. Admiral de Ternay's fleet was anchored in a defensive position and guns were mounted on shore. The British hovered near but did not attack. Rochambeau almost regretted it. In his memoirs he wrote that he was "in the position of hoping for the arrival of General Clinton, rather than fearing his visit."

But Clinton, after his capture of Charleston, had returned to the safety of New York, surrounded by some 15,000 troops. Nearby, at White Plains and then at Dobbs Ferry, Washington held together his lean and tattered army. Unable to leave, he sent Lafayette as his emissary to Rochambeau. This seemed logical to Washington since they spoke the same language. It did not occur to either him or Lafayette that it was not the most tactful thing to do, considering their relative rank.

Had Rochambeau been as full of self-importance as some generals, he would certainly have been furious at the way this mere youth put pressure on him to liberate New York without delay. As it was he was wise enough to recognize Lafayette's zeal and good intentions. Concealing his annoyance, he patiently explained that their eight battleships had no chance against a British Navy three times larger, and pressed for a meeting with Washington. Lafayette sweetly apologized for offending him but then deluged him with more lengthy memoranda on the same subject. Rochambeau replied with a remarkable letter:

> My dear Marquis . . . Let me tell you a great secret which I have learned after forty years of experience. There are no troops more easily beaten than those who have lost confidence in their leaders, and they lose confidence as soon as they see that their lives are being risked to satisfy somebody's personal ambition. . . . And please remember that it is always old Papa Rochambeau who is talking to his dear son, Lafayette, whom he loves, and will continue to love and esteem to his last breath.

Late in August Rochambeau received a delegation of nineteen Oneida Indian warriors who had sided with France

58

during the French and Indian War. He invited them to dinner and gave them medals of Louis XVI's coronation. In turn they presented their hosts with sandals, belts, and "some scalps."

The chief asked Rochambeau: "How is it that the king of France, our father, sends his troops to protect the Americans against the king of England, their father?"

Rochambeau explained as best he could that his king was helping the Americans protect their natural liberties.

The first meeting between him and Washington, in Hartford on September 21, was a personal success. They met as equals and became friends. Washington spoke frankly of the difficulty of recruiting men in a country grown tired of war and of the penniless state of Congress. Rochambeau accepted Washington's problems as his own and assumed no airs of superiority.

Rochambeau's worldly staff officers wholeheartedly idolized the American general. "His face is handsome and majestic but at the same time kind and gentle, corresponding completely with his moral qualities," wrote Comte Axel de Fersen. The Chevalier de Chastellux was even more lyrical: "Brave without temerity, laborious without ambition, generous without prodigality, noble without pride, virtuous without severity, it will be said of him at the end of a long civil war, he has nothing with which he could reproach himself."

George Washington

After the Hartford conference, with its decision to postpone the attack on New York, Rochambeau hastened back to Newport, where he sent his son on a fast frigate with an appeal to the king for more troops, more battleships, and more money for running expenses. It was clearer to him than ever that additional support was essential, if he was to be of any real help to the American cause.

The French settled down for a long wait. At his own expense Rochambeau restored buildings partially destroyed by the British to serve as winter quarters for his troops. He and his officers were quartered in private houses. They were very popular and were invited everywhere. The officers found the young women of Newport "fresh and pretty." There were some romances.

The Chevalier de Chastellux held a dinner for Ezra Stiles, president of Yale College, served "in a splendid manner on thirty-five dishes." Rochambeau and Dr. Stiles talked Latin together. He spoke it tolerably well, Dr. Stiles wrote in his diary and said of his French hosts: "They are as large and as likely men as can be produced in any nation."

59

The Duc de Lauzun and his cavalry were moved to Lebanon, Connecticut, for the winter. Lauzun complained it was like Siberia, "a few huts dispersed in immense forests," but all of them enjoyed the squirrel hunting, and Lauzun got along splendidly with the Lebanon farmers.

In November, Admiral de Ternay died of a mysterious fever. His second in command, the Chevalier des Touches, took charge of the fleet temporarily. Several frigates arrived in January and February, 1781, bringing supplies and money, but Rochambeau scanned the horizon vainly for the second expeditionary force.

He had other troubles. His officers, restless from inaction, criticized him behind his back. The Tories of Newport published an article accusing the French of having "taken possession of Rhode Island in the name of the King of France," and of planning to seize more territory. Merchants and storekeepers, possessed of what he called a "sacred veneration of money," overcharged him constantly. Through all his frustrations Rochambeau remained outwardly imperturbable.

In March, Washington paid them a visit. Rochambeau paraded his troops in the general's honor. In their spotless white uniforms, trimmed with the rainbow colors of their various regiments, they made a dazzling spectacle.

Rochambeau's son did not return until May. Admiral de Barras, their new navy commander, was with him, and they brought part of a gift of 6,000,000 livres, arranged by Benjamin Franklin, for Washington's disposal. Less welcome was their news that the king had vetoed a second expeditionary force. Rochambeau would have been completely disheartened except for a sealed letter from the minister of war. The minister wrote that Admiral Paul de Grasse, who was in charge of a powerful squadron in the West Indies, had been instructed to proceed to America to participate in "any enterprise you may wish to undertake."

At their second conference, held in Wetherfield, Connecticut, on May 21, Rochambeau and Washington discussed this new development. With Admiral de Grasse's fleet they would at last be strong enough to launch an attack against the British, either at New York, or at Chesapeake Bay, where Lafayette was harassing the troops of Cornwallis. Washington favored New York, and Rochambeau yielded with reservations. Washington wrote to General John Sullivan about the forthcoming attack on New York. Spies intercepted the letter and sent it to General Clinton. As it turned out, nothing

60

could have been more fortunate for the French and American allies.

Rochambeau's letters to Admiral de Grasse, sent by fast frigate, spoke frankly of the difficulties of the American armies in the north and the south and mentioned the alternatives of Chesapeake Bay and New York. He reasoned that he had no right to dictate to the admiral where to come. Only de Grasse could know whether his ships, which drew more water than the British ones, could cross Sandy Hook to gain entrance to New York Harbor. Hopefully, Rochambeau also asked the admiral to bring 3000 troops and 1,200,000 livres.

On June 9, the French troops began moving out of Newport to join Washington at Dobbs Ferry, leaving only 600 grenadiers with Admiral de Barras to guard Newport harbor. After eleven months of inactivity, the march through the lovely New England countryside was a tonic. Comte Alexandre Berthier made maps, both accurate and artistic. Americans in the thousands visited their camps. The French bands played and there was dancing. No enemy appeared to stop them although they were within ten miles of British outposts when they reached Washington's camp.

The Continental Army was unbelievably shabby compared to his own troops, but Rochambeau noted that the Americans seemed "very cheerful and healthy," and that about a fourth of them were Negroes, "merry, confident, and sturdy." Abbé Robin, who was with the Soissonnais regiment, was "greatly astonished" that American soldiers had

Interior of a prison ship.

61

less than forty pounds of baggage and that hardly any had mattresses. But he liked their fringed hunting tunics and felt that their "linen pantaloons" were far more practical than the heavier materials of the French.

Washington's army at this time totaled 5835 men, only a few hundred more than their French allies. They could not risk open battle but there were some forays. The Americans discovered that the French, for all their fine uniforms, were good fighters, and the French learned that the ragged Americans were brave to recklessness.

French officers took pleasure in inviting the Americans to share their fine cuisine. The two Berthier brothers and the Chevalier de Lameth made their bivouac beneath a magnificent tulip tree and entertained Washington with an excellent lunch and "Madeira wine and punch." The officers of the Bourbonnais regiment gave a dinner for the officers of the Virginia regiment, serving delicious soup and roast beef. In those warm summer weeks, a feeling of good fellowship arose.

On August 15, Rochambeau heard from Admiral de Grasse. The admiral had received his letters and was acting accordingly. He was bringing 3000 infrantrymen from the West Indies detachment. He was bringing the 1,200,000 livres Rochambeau had requested. He was bringing siege mortars and field artillery. He would arrive by the end of August but would have to be back in the West Indies by mid-October. All he asked was that he be employed promptly and effectively. But he was heading, not for New York, but for Chesapeake Bay!

Faced with this decisive letter, Washington renounced his preference for attacking New York. Preparations were soon under way to move the two armies south, with great precautions so as not to arouse the suspicions of General Clinton. To give the impression they were planning on a long stay, Rochambeau even ordered the building of four huge ovens for making bread. He sent word to Admiral de Barras to join De Grasse in the Chesapeake with his fleet, their siege guns, and 1500 barrels of salt beef stored at Newport. The evacuation took place so quietly it was three days before Clinton knew they were gone. By then troops were parading through Philadelphia with flags flying and bands playing.

From Philadelphia, Washington rode on to Chester, while Rochambeau went by boat along the Delaware. When the boat pulled up to the Chester dock on September 5, he saw the dignified General Washington standing waving wildly, a broad smile on his face. As soon as Rochambeau stepped down the gangplank, Washington excitedly told him that Admiral de Grasse's fleet had reached the Chesapeake safely; a messenger had just brought the news!

They still had the problem of transporting their more than 10,000 men the rest of the way. Boats were found to ship some from the northern end of the long Chesapeake Bay; the others had to go on foot. Washington, with the zeal of a young man, rode ahead of the others to have a three-day visit at his home in Mount Vernon. By the time Rochambeau and his staff reached there, the general's wife, Martha, had prepared a huge repast, a small return for the French hospitality so generously bestowed on the Americans.

At dawn on September 12, the generals with their staff set out on the last lap on their journey. They had not gone far when a horseman rode up to them. He had come from Lafayette to let them know that Admiral de Grasse had abandoned his blockade at the mouth of the Chesapeake. A British fleet had appeared and the French had gone out to sea after it. There had been smoke and sounds of gunfire and then both fleets had disappeared. No one knew the outcome of the battle, nor was there any sign of Admiral de Barras's smaller fleet, which should have arrived.

Once again their carefully laid plans were in jeopardy. Rochambeau and Washington did not need to put their doubts and fears into words. They could only continue on their way, hoping for the best.

Le Comte Paul de Grasse

Paul de Grasse

I have read with great sadness of the distress in which the Americans find themselves and the necessity of the prompt aid which you request.

A favorite tourist spot in France is the picturesque town of Grasse, which lies in the hills above the Riviera in the *département* of Alpes-Maritimes. Grasse is famous for its manufacture of perfumes and is set in vast plantations of jasmine, tuberoses, lavender, lilies of the valley, and carnations. The contrasting colors delight the eye and the blending fragrances drench the spirit.

In the feudal château of Bar, six miles from this town which bears his family name, François Joseph Paul, Comte de Grasse, was born in 1722. His family, of ancient Provençal nobility, traced their lineage back to AD 993.

As a boy, he was tall, athletic, and headstrong. At eleven, his father enrolled him in the Marine Seminary at Toulon, a Jesuit school which prepared young noblemen to become naval officers. As a student Guard of the Marine, de Grasse wore a long-tailed blue woolen coat lined with scarlet serge; scarlet cuffs, vest, knee breeches, and silk stockings; a blue cocked hat trimmed with gold lace; and gold epaulets. He was so diligent in his studies that at the end of his first year he was one of the select few chosen to continue their studies as pages under the Grand Master of the Knights of St. John on the island of Malta.

The school of Malta was both expensive and exclusive. To be eligible, a page had to have four patents of nobility on his father's side and three on his mother's. Young Paul wore an even more elaborate uniform than at Toulon, including a hat with high white plumes and shoes with high red heels. His superior, the Chevalier Jacques François de Chambray, had fought thirty-one naval engagements, captured eleven ships and 400,000 livres of booty.

After their first two years pages were assigned to duty on Maltese ships, which cruised the Mediterranean to protect merchantmen against Corsairs, Turks, and pirates. There is a story that on one of these cruises young Paul de Grasse became angry at a sailor who refused to obey orders, tossed him bodily across the deck—and then ran and picked him up to make sure he was not hurt.

At eighteen, after six years of apprenticeship on Malta, he left to enlist in the French Navy. In 1742, a year after the War of the Austrian Succession (1741–1748) broke out, he took part in a sea battle against the British. (Rochambeau was serving in the French Army in this same war.) For three hours the French flagship, the 40-gun *Gloire,* exchanged blasts of cannon fire with the British flagship *Prince George.* The *Gloire's* captain was decapitated by a cannonball. Ensign de Grasse, standing near him, was severely wounded. Eventually the French had to surrender, but their captors congratulated them on their heroism. De Grasse with the other prisoners of war was taken to England and held for three months. He learned a good deal about the British Navy there and made some English friends.

On furlough in 1754, he returned to Malta, joined the order of the Knights of St. John, and spent two years as an officer of the Maltese fleet. He was back in the French Navy for the Seven Years' War, serving as a ship captain across the seas from the West Indies to India.

The year after the war ended, at the age of forty-two, he fell in love, for the first time in his life, with Antoinette Rosalie Accaron, the beautiful daughter of Louis XV's *valet de chambre.* For her he defied his family, who disapproved because her social standing was lower than their own, and gave up his membership as a Knight of Malta, since that order required a vow of celibacy. Their marriage took place at Versailles in the presence of the king and queen. Seven years later, in 1773, De Grasse's wife died, leaving one son and four daughters. This was the year the Americans tossed cargoes of tea into Boston harbor.

The British had practically annihilated the French Navy in the Seven Years' War, but ever since they had rested on their laurels. Louis XV's foreign minister, the Duc de Choiseul, set French shipwrights to work turning out three-deck battleships. Soon they were building them in half the time it took the British to build similar ships.

To provide French ship captains with the skills of their British rivals, Admiral Sieur d'Orvilliers took a fleet on a four-month training cruise. De Grasse was captain of the corvette *Isis.* D'Orvilliers called him the most highly skilled captain in the squadron: "Although his vessel was inferior in quality, he gave to the maneuvers all the precision and brilliance possible."

The British, through spies, knew all about France's efforts to improve her navy but did not take them seriously. The French were "land animals," they said. They would never be at home on the seas.

The first real test came on July 27, 1778, four months after the Franco-American treaty, in a sea battle near the island of Ouessant off the coast of Brittany. Twenty-seven French ships opposed thirty British ones. De Grasse, still under Admiral d'Orvilliers, had charge of the fleet's second division. After severe fighting, the battle ended indecisively with neither side able to claim victory, but the fact that the French had been able to stand up to the larger British fleet was proof that British supremacy was already in question.

From the beginning of this renewed struggle with England, France vigorously pursued a campaign in the West Indies to protect her valuable "sugar islands." On March 28, 1781, de Grasse was given the title of admiral and ordered to the West Indies to take charge of this operation, in cooperation with their Spanish allies, who were protecting *their* West Indies islands.

He set sail with a fleet of twenty battleships and a convoy of 150 merchant ships. His flagship was the 110-gun *Ville de Paris,* the largest and finest battleship in the world, a gift

The sea battle near Ouessant.

French officers in Philadelphia.

of the city of Paris to the French nation. He had with him instructions to detach part of his fleet and go on to America later in the summer to cooperate with Generals Washington and Rochambeau, should they so desire.

This was the first time de Grasse had commanded a fleet, though he had risen steadily in rank over the years and had long been accustomed to authority. At fifty-seven, he was a big handsome well-built man with an imposing manner. "An exceedingly brave officer, honorable and proud," one of his own officers described him. His sailors said simply that though he measured six feet two, on battle days he was six feet six.

Admiral de Grasse's opponent in the West Indies was Sir George Rodney, England's most talented admiral. Rodney commanded a fleet of twenty-one battleships. De Grasse sighted the island of Martinique on April 28. Had Rodney with his full fleet attacked him then, when he was encumbered with a huge convoy, the results might have been disastrous. Luckily for the French, Rodney was detained on the tiny island of Eustatius, which he had recently captured from the Dutch, and sent his second in command, Sir Samuel Hood, with a mere fifteen ships, to meet de Grasse. The two fleets sparred a little and then Hood retreated. De Grasse moved into Martinique's Fort Royal Harbor (now Fort de France), where four more battleships were waiting for him. De Grasse's fleet now outnumbered the British one. All that spring the French were on the offensive. Among their victories was the capture of the island of Tobago, which produced large quantities of indigo.

De Grasse returned to Martinique on June 18 and found three letters from General Rochambeau awaiting him, asking for money, artillery, and troops, and leaving to the admiral's discretion whether he should come to Chesapeake Bay or New York. On reading them carefully, and perhaps reading between the lines, De Grasse determined that the Chesapeake should be his destination.

It was a matter of pride with him to meet all Rochambeau's requests. He persuaded the French Colonial Governor of Saint-Domingue (Haiti) to release 3000 French infantrymen, under the Marquis de Saint-Simon, as well as cannon, siege guns, and mortars. Saint-Simon was in truth delighted with this arrangement since his men had been suffering from the tropical climate. The only condition was that they must be back in time for the winter campaign.

Finding money was more difficult. The French colonial treasury was empty. De Grasse and one of his captains offered to put up as security their large plantations in Saint-Domingue, to which de Grasse added his beloved Château of Tilly in France, but no banker or private citizen would give them a penny on these properties, for reasons that have never been made clear. As a last resort, the admiral turned to the Spanish director general of customs, Señor de Salavedro, who agreed to try to raise the money in Havana. He was successful. The wealthy Spanish colonists of Havana, more patriotic or more generous than the French colonists, were glad to help. Their wives offered their diamonds.

All these steps were taken by de Grasse on his own initiative. Also on his own initiative, and contrary to his instructions, he decided to take his entire fleet to America rather than detaching a few ships. In addition he spent a large part of his personal fortune to charter fifteen merchant ships to transport equipment and field artillery for the Marquis de Saint-Simon's troops! This personal sacrifice de Grasse made for the American cause has received scant mention in history. It was all the more amazing in that, unlike Lafayette, he had never been imbued with the glory of the American fight for freedom. His first loyalty was to France. He did only what seemed normal to him in this war which France and America were fighting side by side.

In the meantime General Clinton had written Admiral Rodney to bring his fleet to New York, where he thought an attack was imminent. Rodney had finished his affairs on Eustatius island but he was now suffering from gout. He ordered Sir Samuel Hood to take fourteen battleships and follow Admiral de Grasse, who he believed was heading for New York, but with only part of his fleet. Then, confident that he had done everything possible, he sailed for England to recover his health.

Late in July the French fleet suffered two freak accidents. The ship's clerk on the *Intrépide* went into the cockpit to draw the ration of brandy served sailors with their breakfast, upset

Sir Henry Clinton, commander of the British forces in North America.

his lantern, and started a fire. Twenty sailors died by drowning when they jumped into the sea to escape the flames. A few days afterwards a fire started on the *Inconstante* in an almost identical manner. One hundred and twenty sailors perished. Admiral de Grasse decreed that henceforth only officers would be authorized to distribute brandy.

Even with these losses, a fleet of twenty-eight battleships set sail on August 5, in addition to the frigates and transport ships. The British did not catch a glimpse of this impressive fleet. Instead of following the usual Atlantic route north, the admiral directed his captains to pass through the Bahama Channel, a treacherous ten-mile belt of water between Cuba and Bahama.

In spite of contrary winds and threatening reefs, there was only one near-accident, when the helmsman of a 74-gun ship gave the wheel a wrong turn and she ran into the breakers. On August 17, they rendezvoused with the frigate *Aigrette* from Havana, which brought them the promised 1,200,000 livres in gold. De Grasse could now send word ahead to Rochambeau on a fast frigate that all his demands were met. From then on they were in open waters and safe.

On the calm evening of August 29, the French fleet arrived at the mouth of Chesapeake Bay. A boat came from shore carrying a Tory. "Which vessel is Lord Rodney's flagship?" he called to them. That was when de Grasse was sure the British knew nothing of his voyage. A crew member who spoke English invited the stranger aboard and they confiscated his cargo. It consisted of some excellent melons and other delicacies, which they consumed in honor of Rodney.

Soon they were anchored within the bay, blocking off Lord Cornwallis from a sea route of escape. The Marquis de Saint-Simon debarked his 3000 troops, who left to join Lafayette at Williamsburg.

There was no sign of Admiral Hood's fleet and for good reason. He had sailed by the direct route and reached the Chesapeake five days before de Grasse. When he saw that the bay was empty he went on to New York to join Admiral Graves, who was in charge of the British navy in America. Graves knew nothing of the whereabouts of de Grasse, though he had learned that Admiral de Barras had left Newport for the Chesapeake with eight battleships. The combined British fleets set out after him, confident they could easily destroy the smaller fleet. They reached Chesapeake Bay on the morning of September 5 to find not the de Barras fleet, but the twenty-eight battleships of de Grasse.

As soon as Admiral de Grasse sighted his enemy, he ordered his captains to clear their ships for action, slip cables, attach their anchors to the buoys and prepare to move out into the open sea for the battle he knew was inevitable. Some 2000 of his seamen were ashore collecting wood and water for the fleet, too far away to signal. They had to be left behind. It was almost noon before the ships were under way.

The French had only one more battleship than the British but they carried 2000 cannon while the British had only 1500. The British had the advantage of the wind, which was from the north-northeast. Their ships were copper-bottomed which gave them greater maneuverability, and in addition they were fully manned. In accordance with eighteenth-century naval practice, their ships stretched in a single line, bowsprit to stern. The huge cannon that lined the three-deckers of both fleets, starboard and port side, could fire only broadside.

The French fleet, hampered by the winds, had difficulty getting into position. For an hour or more, their foremost ships, the van, were far ahead of the center and rear ships. Because it was inconsistent with his naval training, Admiral Graves missed his chance to cut off these van ships and destroy them before the others brought up support, for which he was later severely criticized. By 3:45 P.M. the two opposing vans and center ships were roughly parallel, though the rear ships of both fleets were miles apart.

The French on these van ships could clearly see their opponent on the British lead ship, the *Shrewsbury*—the gunners, the powder boys sitting on boxes of high explosives, the gun captains with boxes of explosive priming powder buckled at their waists, the officers in blue-and-gold uniforms standing by their divisions with drawn swords, and the captain on the quarterdeck in the most exposed position of all. On the English ships as on the French, the entire crew was on deck and hatches were fastened down so no one would be tempted to bolt to safety.

At 4:03 P.M., Admiral Graves gave the order to fire and the French responded. Cannon roared. There was the screech of crashing masts, of splintering hulls, and the shrieks of the wounded. Smoke and fire soared toward the skies and blood stained the decks.

The *Réfléchi* received a broadside from the British *Princessa*, which killed her captain and wounded another officer. The *Diadem* fought several British ships at one time and everyone aboard her was killed, wounded, or burned. The *Auguste,* under Commodore de Bougainville, suffered fifty-four hits in her hull and seventy in her sails and had her foretop bowline shot off. Two sailors in turn attempted to repair it and both were wounded. Bougainville offered his purse for any volunteer who would try a third time. A sailor tackled the job successfully but refused the purse. "My General, we do not go there for money," he said.

The terrible battle lasted for more than two hours. At 6:30 dusk fell and the cannon were silent. Much as the French had suffered, the damage to the British fleet was far worse. Of the human casualties, the British had 90 killed and 246 wounded; the total French casualties were 209.

This naval battle, known as the Battle of Virginia Capes, was the largest and most important in the American Revolution, and one in which, oddly enough, not a single American was engaged.

All the next day the carpenters and riggers of both fleets were busy making repairs. They did their job so well that not a single ship was lost, except the British *Terrible,* which had been in poor shape before the battle began. Her pumps were blown and when finally she began taking water at the rate of eight feet an hour, the crew stripped her of powder and supplies and set fire to her.

For the following three days the two fleets kept in sight of each other, moving southeast from Chesapeake Bay. Each

Model of the 100-gun flagship Ville de Paris.

73

side watched for an attack from the other, but did not initiate it. On September 9, Admiral de Grasse sighted some sails to the north. He assumed, correctly, that this was the fleet of Admiral de Barras from Newport, and maneuvered to keep between it and the British fleet.

That night the British set sail for New York to complete their repairs. It was their acknowledgment of defeat. The French circled back to the Chesapeake. The first thing they saw on arrival was the sails of Admiral de Barras's fleet, which had slipped into the bay unnoticed by the British. Once more Lord Cornwallis was solidly blockaded.

In the following days, Admiral de Grasse was besieged with requests by the allied troops on shore for every type of supplies. When finally he received a demand for thirty candles for the artillery, he exploded: "Damn it! You have stretched the blanket too tight." Shortly afterward he wrote to apologize to General Rochambeau: "I am a Provençal and a sailor, which is enough to entitle me to a quick temper, and I acknowledge my fault and trust in your friendship."

By this time he had already entertained Rochambeau and General Washington aboard his flagship, the *Ville de Paris.*

Washington, by Rembrandt Peale.

The Yorktown Siege

"Oh God, it is all over! it is all over! it is all over!"
—British Prime Minister LORD NORTH, *on
learning of the surrender of* CORNWALLIS

*W*hen Rochambeau and Washington rode into Williamsburg on September 14, 1781, drums were beating to announce their arrival, and the tree-lined streets were filled with soldiers, French and American. Lafayette had been ill with a fever, but he rose from his sickbed, dressed, and dashed out to kiss General Washington heartily on both cheeks in the French manner. There were plenty of other generals around too: gallant Anthony Wayne, stout Henry Knox, the Prussian Baron von Steuben, Benjamin Lincoln, still smoldering from the humiliating surrender of Charleston, and the Marquis Claude Saint-Simon, who had come with Admiral de Grasse.

The cloud of uncertainty as to the fate of de Grasse's fleet was dispersed the next day, when a scout reported that it had returned to the Chesapeake after inflicting a stunning defeat

*The Capitol at
Williamsburg*

on the British. The worries about Admiral de Barras were over too. After leaving Newport, he had taken his small fleet far out to sea to avoid the British, but now his ships, too, were safely in the bay. In Yorktown, twelve miles away, General Cornwallis, reportedly busy with his defenses, had made no effort to move out nor did he even seem aware of his desperate situation.

Later that day Admiral de Grasse sent a captured British ship, the *Queen Charlotte,* up the James River, with an invitation to Washington and Rochambeau to visit him on the *Ville de Paris.* The *Queen Charlotte* brought them and their general staffs to the flagship on September 17. The fleet guns fired a salute as they stepped aboard. Admiral de Grasse stood waiting to welcome them in a blue and scarlet uniform decorated with gold lace and the wide flame-colored ribbon of the Order of St. Louis diagonally across his chest.

There is a legend that the tall admiral strode forward, hugged the equally tall Washington, and exclaimed, "My little general!" to the amusement of Henry Knox and the others of the party. More likely the American general and the French admiral greeted each other with all the formal dignity that the occasion demanded.

In de Grasse's private cabin, Washington had the chance to thank the admiral for his timely aid, and obligingly de Grasse agreed to extend his stay two weeks beyond his limit of October 15 if necessary, once more risking the displeasure of his superiors. Their conference was followed by a dinner of many courses and many bottles of good French wine, during which toasts were drunk to Louis XVI, to Congress, and to American independence. Later the admiral took his guests for a tour of the flagship. They were particularly impressed with the beautiful flowers and tropical plants which seemed literally to grow between cannons. At sunset the fleet guns gave them a farewell salute as the generals and their party left on the *Queen Charlotte.*

The return journey was less pleasant. Because of bad weather, it took four wearisome days. Troops and supplies were still arriving on boats and barges along the James River. The next several days were spent in unloading and checking the supplies and reorganizing their forces, which for once outnumbered the enemy more than three to one. Under Cornwallis were an estimated 8800 troops and around a thousand Negroes, who had fled to the British on the promise of freedom. The allies had, in addition to the militia, approximately 8300 Continental Army and 7500 French troops,

19,000 seamen under de Grasse and 5000 in Admiral de Barras's squadron.

The three divisions of the Continental forces were commanded by Lafayette, Baron von Steuben, and General Benjamin Lincoln. Rochambeau and the Marquis de Saint-Simon commanded their own French regiments. The militia, mostly from Virginia, were under General Thomas Nelson, Jr., and Brigadier General Weedon.

Before dawn on September 28, the allies began the march to Yorktown, twelve miles down the peninsula. The drums beat a resounding march. The Americans held the right of the line, while the French were on the left. Some English dragoons rode up to challenge them, but two companies of French *grenadiers* and *chasseurs* (light infantry) under Baron de Vioménil drove them off. Vioménil's *grenadiers* and *chasseurs* were the advance guard and as they approached Yorktown they spread out to form a semicircle around it.

This object of so much concentrated military and naval power was a hamlet of only about sixty or so buildings, set on a high bluff above the York river and protected on two sides by swamps. Most of its citizens, staunch American patriots, had left at the outbreak of the war. Once it had been a prosperous tobacco port and it still had some fine houses. As his headquarters, Cornwallis had commandeered Governor Nelson's home, a large and handsome mansion, to which, according to one visitor, "neither European taste nor luxury was denied." Seventy-year-old Thomas Nelson, Sr., still lived there. Though he had two sons in the rebel armies, he had taken no sides in the struggle. Cornwallis treated the old man courteously and let him go and come as he liked.

77

General Charles Cornwallis, Sixth Earl of Eyre

To the French and American allies, this General Charles Cornwallis, Sixth Earl of Eyre, symbolized "the enemy." In fact, he was a man of many sterling qualities. As a member of the House of Lords before the war, he had strongly opposed Parliament's taxing of the American colonies, but much as he sympathized with their grievances he considered the armed rebellion an act of treason. He had fought the rebels since 1776 and was at this time in charge of British armies in the south, but still under General Clinton.

His seeming retreat to the Chesapeake before Lafayette's troops had in fact been the result of a direct order. Clinton had instructed Cornwallis to send 2000 men to New York for the attack he expected there and Cornwallis had headed for the coast where transport could be found for them. Later Clinton wrote him to send the troops to Philadelphia instead of New York, and after that had changed his mind again and ordered him to send no troops but to set up a defensive post on the York River. Cornwallis had selected Yorktown as the best site, though wearily he had written Clinton that such defenses would be "a work of great time and labour and after all, I fear, not be very strong." His opinion of Clinton's generalship was understandably not very high.

During August and September, with the aid of Negro labor, the British fortified Yorktown. The inner defenses were strong and secure, bristling with cannon and long pine spears designed to impale anyone rash enough to charge them. The outer line was never completed, for they did not have the needed tools. The day after the allies surrounded him, Cornwallis abandoned the outer defenses. Clinton had now promised to send a fleet to support Cornwallis, and he reasoned he could hold out within the inner defenses until the ships arrived. (The fleet did not appear until October 22, when it was too late.)

For the allies, an open attack on Yorktown would have meant overwhelming casualties. A siege was necessary, and siege tactics were unfamiliar to the Americans. Washington turned to General Rochambeau and Baron von Steuben for advice. They explained the siege tactics of the French master in military science, Sébastien Le Prestre de Vauban (1633–1707), who had served under Louis XIV.

Vauban's strategy was to dig a series of parallel trenches, connected with zigzag trenches through which artillery could be brought up within shooting range and installed in redoubts, or small fortifications. Thus the enemy defenses could be seriously weakened, or even destroyed, before an open attack.

Yorktown from the French encampment.

Preliminary work on the trenches began immediately, under the direction of two French engineers, Messieurs de Vernon and de Memonville. French and American soldiers worked together stripping trees to make *fascines,* bundles of sticks used to strengthen the walls of redoubts; *saucissons* (sausages in English), which were like the *fascines* only larger; *gabions,* wickerwork baskets filled with earth to support embankments; and *fraises,* pointed sticks to be driven into the embankments in upright or slanted positions. Because of the sandy soil around Yorktown, a huge supply of these items was needed to keep the trenches firm.

The British, many of whom were crack shots, shelled them steadily with cannon and mortar. One American officer noted that on October 2 the British had fired 352 shots. The allies were under orders not to return the fire but to save their ammunition until later. Seamen transported heavy artillery and siege guns from the two French fleets on small craft up the James River. General Henry Knox had the responsibility of bringing the artillery across the peninsula to their camps by commandeered oxteams, by horses borrowed from the officers, and by manpower.

To the distress of his aides, Washington made the rounds of the front lines daily, oblivious to the danger. Both he and Rochambeau were worried lest Cornwallis and his men should try to escape to Gloucester, directly across the York River, on the ships anchored along the riverbank. Every morning at dawn Rochambeau's aides scrambled down to the river to check on these ships, invariably drawing a volley of musketry.

At Gloucester, Cornwallis had stationed General Banastre Tarleton's dragoons, who were raiding the countryside for

80

Yorktown from the American sector.

whatever they could find. General Weedon and his Virginia militia were posted around Gloucester to try to stop them, but when their forces proved insufficient General Rochambeau sent over the Duc de Lauzun and his legion of cavalry. The daring assignment was very much to their taste and they hounded the dragoons until eventually, for lack of fodder, Tarleton had to kill a thousand horses.

An American Negro in Lafayette's service, known simply as James, managed at great peril to enter the British camp and bring back valuable information. For his contribution he was later freed and took for himself the name of James Lafayette.

The digging of the first parallel took place the night of October 6. It was in the form of a slightly curved trench, 800 to 1000 yards south and southwest of the British defenses, stretching over a thousand yards from the riverbank. The Bourbonnais and the Soissonnais French regiments supplied a thousand diggers. The rest were Americans. *Gabines* and *fascines* were piled along the line of the trench on the side toward the enemy. As the men dug they flung dirt over them, so that a long parapet arose.

At dawn the British gunners discovered the earthworks and started shooting, but the parapets protected the men in the trenches. All that day and the next the diggers constructed artillery batteries and platforms for the powerful French siege guns. They built and strengthened four redoubts, two on each end of the parallel. Morale was high. Men started betting their beaver caps on how many days it would take before Cornwallis surrendered. Their work was interrupted only when a sentry called out, "Shell!" whereupon everyone dropped flat in the trench.

The French finished their batteries first, and at 3:00 P.M. on October 9 Washington granted them permission to open fire on the British ships whose gunners had so frequently harassed them. At 5:00 P.M., Washington put the match to the touchhole to send the first cannonball hurtling into Yorktown. Then the bombardment began in earnest. French and Americans poured mortar shells into the town and fired *à ricochet,* to send cannonballs skipping across the ground and up against the British batteries. Enemy cannon were their principal target. All night long they continued, so as to prevent the British from repairing their damaged batteries. The French siege guns were a surprise to Cornwallis; he had thought the Americans had only a few pieces of field artillery.

About noon on October 10 the British sent up a flag of truce and old Mr. Nelson hobbled from the besieged town. Cornwallis had granted his release at the request of Washington. In Washington's tent the old man told them that his home, headquarters of Cornwallis, was in ruins. The British general and his chief officers had taken refuge in a grotto at the foot of the garden; others had sought shelter in caves in the riverbank.

The French gunners launched more attacks on British ships that night, using cannonballs heated to an almost molten state and starting fires on the frigate *Charon* and two transports. The next day the British towed their remaining ships over to Gloucester.

During all this firing, French and American fatigue troops were digging zigzag trenches forward to within 360 yards of
Washington at Yorktown the enemy parapets. By the evening of October 11, nearly

all the British guns were silenced. As soon as it was dark French engineers laid out the line of the second parallel, and diggers with shovels, spades, hoes, and *fascines,* and accompanied by armed guards, crept forward and began digging. A spy had informed on them. Some British guns opened fire on diggers from the French Gâtinais and Royal Deux-Ponts regiments. They returned the fire and then all was quiet again.

The second parallel could not be completed that night because the British had constructed two redoubts, known as No. 9 and No. 10, which were directly in the path of the parallel. Diggers stopped their work about 250 yards from these redoubts.

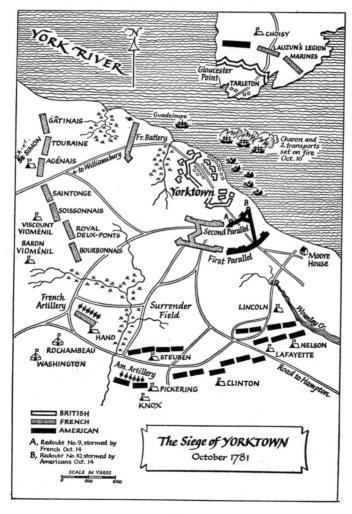

The Siege of YORKTOWN
October 1781

BRITISH
FRENCH
AMERICAN

A, Redoubt No. 9, stormed by French Oct. 14
B, Redoubt No. 10, stormed by Americans Oct. 14

SCALE IN YARDS
0   500   1000

Lafayette, Washington, and Rochambeau during the siege of Yorktown.

These redoubts had to be captured if the siege plan was to be successful. General Washington assigned Redoubt No. 10 to the Americans, under Lafayette. He appointed his former aide, Major de Gimat, to lead the assault, but young Alexander Hamilton was so eager to have the honor of risking his life that he persuaded General Washington to let him take de Gimat's place, on the ground that it was his tour of duty.

Redoubt No. 9, which was larger and more strongly fortified, was left to the French to take. Rochambeau assigned Colonel William de Deux-Ponts to lead the assault. Among his troops were about 400 men from the Gâtinais regiment, which Rochambeau had commanded in the Seven Years' War, when it was still called the Auvergne regiment. The name had been changed arbitrarily and the men resented it. As they marched past Rochambeau, he called out, *"Auvergne, sans tache!"* (Auvergne, the unblemished!) The men shouted back to him that if he would restore their ancient and honored name they would fight "like lions until the last man is killed."

"I have great need of you tonight, my children," he told them, promising that if they succeeded he would go to the king himself to have the name Auvergne restored.

The watchword for the allies was "Rochambeau," which the Americans pronounced most appropriately as "Rush-on-Boys." As the French mounted their redoubt they

84

shouted, *"Vive le Roi"* (Long live the king), a curious battle cry indeed for an army fighting for freedom from monarchy.

The assaults on the two redoubts began that night at eight. The British fought bravely but vainly. The Americans took Redoubt No. 10 in exactly ten minutes, with total casualties of thirty-four. It took the French thirty minutes to capture Redoubt No. 9. Their casualties amounted to ninety-two. By the next morning both redoubts were part of the second parallel and the allies were constructing batteries for the final attack.

A massive close-range bombardment was soon under way. The French guns were so accurate that their gunners were able to hit the same embrasure—the recess from which cannon were fired—six out of seven shots. Dr. James Thatcher of Massachusetts noted that "the whole peninsula trembles under the incessant thunder of our infernal machines." By October 15, not a single British cannon answered them. In Yorktown there was no safe place. Shells rained down even on their hospitals where there were hundreds of sick and wounded.

Fight for the British redoubts at Yorktown.

Cornwallis had not yet given up. At 3:00 A.M. on the morning of October 16, picked British troops moved stealthily into the parallel between the French and American troops. Before they were driven back they had spiked some of the cannon by ramming their bayonets into the cannon touch-holes. Though they lacked time to do an efficient job of spiking, it took engineers and artillerymen all the next morning to repair the damage. Then the bombardment was renewed, as deadly as ever.

That night Cornwallis did what Rouchambeau and Washington had suspected he might. He attempted to take his men across to Gloucester on large flatboats. This time it was Nature which came to the aid of the Americans. No sooner were the first flatboats under way than a violent thunderstorm drenched them and wind and waves forced them back to Yorktown. At dawn some of the troops were still on the water. From the captured redoubts French and American fire swept over them.

At nine o'clock that morning of October 17, a small English drummer in a bright red coat appeared on top of the ruined British parapet and began vigorously beating his drum. Immediately afterward a British officer walked toward the American lines, waving a white handkerchief. The guns fell silent. The Americans escorted him to their trenches. He gave them a letter from Cornwallis to General Washington:

> Sir: I propose a cessation of hostilities for twenty-four hours, and that two officers may be appointed by each side to meet at Mr. Moore's house to settle terms for the surrender of the posts at York and Gloucester.
> I have the honor to be &c.
> Cornwallis.

On October 19, in Redoubt No. 10, George Washington affixed his signature to the final surrender terms, along with "Le Comte de Rochambeau." Washington had invited de Grasse to join them but he was ill and Admiral de Barras signed for both of them: "Le Comte de Barras in my name and that of the Comte de Grasse."

The surrender ceremony took place in a meadow about half a mile down the Williamsburg road. The French wore their dress uniforms, immaculate as always. On the American side, the Continental soldiers, who had brushed up their shabby uniforms and polished their guns, held the first ranks,

French commanders at Yorktown surrender.

while the militia, who had no uniforms, stayed in the rear. At their head, on horseback, were Washington and his staff. Opposite them were Rochambeau and his staff, also on horseback.

The English army approached from Yorktown, their drums pounding a slow and mournful tune. Cornwallis was not with them. At the last moment he pleaded illness and sent his second in command, General Charles O'Hara. General O'Hara stopped to ask Comte Mathieu Dumas to point out Rochambeau. The French aide did so, and O'Hara rode toward his general. Rochambeau described what happened next. "On arriving, he (General O'Hara) presented his sword to me. I pointed opposite to General Washington, as the head of the American army, and I said that the French army, being auxiliary upon that continent, it was to the American general that he must look for his orders."

Clearly the British felt it would be less humiliating to surrender to the French than to the American rebels, but Rochambeau refused to play their game. Nor would Washington accept the sword from Cornwallis' second in

REDDITION DE L'ARMÉE DU LORD CORNWALLIS

French drawing showing the surrender of Cornwallis at Yorktown.

command, but directed O'Hara to his second in command, General Benjamin Lincoln.

With the surrender of Cornwallis at Yorktown, America's independence was assured, although the final peace treaty was not signed until September 3, 1783. This major battle in American and world history, in which the French played a decisive role, was marked by amazingly small casualties. Thirty Americans were killed exclusive of the militia, whose losses were not recorded, and 100 were wounded. The French had 60 killed and 193 wounded. The British suffered more heavily with 156 killed and 326 wounded. As in all battles before the twentieth century, losses by disease were far more than in actual fighting.

Abbé Robin described how Philadelphia reacted to the news of the fall of Yorktown:

> Echoes of joy were heard from every quarter; some merry fellows mounted on scaffolds and stages, pronounced funeral orations for Cornwallis, and uttered lamentations on the grief and distress of the Tories. People ran in crowds to the residence of the Minister of France and "Long live Louis the Sixteenth!" was the general cry.

As soon as possible Lafayette rushed to Paris to report to his king: "The play is over, the fifth act is finished, the cause of humanity won."

Moore house, Yorktown.

Aftermath

America has given us this example. The act which declared its independence is a simple and sublime exposition of these rights so sacred and so long forgotten.

—ANTOINE-NICOLAS DE CONDORCET, *French philosopher and patriot, writing in 1786*

*I*n after years the French veterans of Yorktown looked back at their stay in America as a romantic and even peaceful interlude. It was, in view of the stormy fate that awaited most of them.

Destiny struck quickly and cruelly on the seemingly invincible Admiral Paul de Grasse. Following the surrender of Cornwallis, he sailed back to the West Indies to join the Spanish in a campaign to capture Jamaica from England. Admiral Rodney, restored to health, was reassigned to that area. In a battle on April 9, 1782, he and his British fleet destroyed most of the French fleet and captured the magnificent *Ville de Paris* and six other vessels. De Grasse was taken prisoner and held in England. He returned to France in disgrace, his contribution at Yorktown forgotten, and spent his last years in retirement.

The American Revolution had cost France 200,000,000 livres in loans, gifts, subsidies, and maintenance of their fleets and armies. At twenty cents a livre, this amounted to approximately $50,000,000, and many times that in modern buying power. This expenditure, not the extravagance of the beautiful Marie Antoinette, wreaked such havoc on the national economy that France became ripe for its revolution, which followed in 1789, six years after the American one ended.

Charles Gravier, Comte de Vergennes, died in 1787 and so missed the realization of his fear that "the spirit of revolt . . . may become contagious." Louis XVI died on the guillotine on January 21, 1793. His queen met the same fate the following October.

General Rochambeau, who had returned from America to receive high honors from his king, continued to serve in the army following the Revolution. In 1794, during the Reign of Terror when anyone of noble birth became suspect and

Louis XVI distributing alms to the poor

many others as well, he was arrested and thrown in prison for six months, escaping the guillotine by a lucky chance. Much later Napoleon appointed him Formal Marshal of France and Grand Officer of the Legion of Honor. He died at the age of eighty, sitting in his armchair.

Diverse fates attended the officers who had served under him. His second in command, Baron de Vioménil, was in charge of the Swiss guards posted at the Palace of the Tuileries where Louis XVI was being held. He lost his life when they were attacked by a Paris mob. Comte Axel Fersen, Rochambeau's Swedish aide-de-camp, planned the daring escape of Marie Antoinette and the king from the Tuileries, which ended dismally in failure. Comte Charles de Damas and Chevalier de Lameth, who had both been wounded at Redoubt No. 9, became fugitives and exiles from their native land. Comte Alexandre Berthier had a fabulous career as Napoleon's most trusted general.

The gallant Duc de Lauzun chose the side of the Revolutionists and fought well for them, but eventually he became suspect and was condemned to the guillotine. The morning of his sentence his executioner found him in his cell dining on oysters and white wine. "Citizen, allow me to finish," he said. Then he offered his glass to the executioner: "Take this wine. You must need courage in your profession."

Pierre Charles L'Enfant

Rochambeau's son, the Vicomte de Rochambeau, made his military career in the West Indies. A lieutenant-general in 1792, he was in command of the Windward Islands. Two years later he surrendered to the British who besieged him in Martinique and eventually was exchanged for General O'Hara, Cornwallis' second in command at Yorktown. Later, as governor of Haiti, he made an unenviable reputation for himself for his cruelty to the Negro population.

Some of the French who had fought in America stayed on, married, and made new lives for themselves. One of them was the painter and architect Pierre Charles L'Enfant, who had served as an engineer in the Continental Army and who later designed the beautifully laid out city of Washington, D.C.

Caron de Beaumarchais bounded up rapidly from the near-bankruptcy in which Hortalez & Company had left him. His *Marriage of Figaro,* after long censorship bans, was played before the Versailles court in 1783 and the next year at the *Comédie Française,* with resounding success. He married for the third time, very happily. There were some new financial ventures, from the profits of which he built a magnificent mansion near the Bastille. Between 1785 and 1790 he devoted himself to publishing a 70-volume edition of the works of Voltaire.

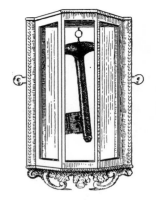

Key to the Bastille

Though he ardently supported the French Revolution, his former connections with Versailles aroused suspicion. In 1792 he was thrown in prison, escaping a death sentence only because of the intervention of a woman who admired him. He fled to Hamburg, where he lived in misery. In his absence his wife and daughter were imprisoned and everything he owned was confiscated. The tide had turned in his favor by the time he returned. He was welcomed as a celebrity, recovered part of his fortune, and lived modestly until his death in 1799. In 1835, Congress finally voted his descendants the minimum sum of 800,000 francs in payment for the stores of supplies which Beaumarchais provided when they were most needed.

In the first years of the French Revolution, Lafayette was recognized as a national leader. He composed the French Declaration of the Rights of Man, based on America's Declaration of Independence. "Men are born and remain free and equal in rights," it read. "Social distinctions may be based only on common utility." It was Lafayette who ordered the destruction of the Bastille, a symbol of tyranny. Later he sent the key of the Bastille to George Washington. Then in 1792 he was denounced and had to flee across the border. In Austria he was captured and imprisoned for five years, part of the time in a subterranean dungeon. Napoleon arranged his release.

In 1824 this aged warrior came to America at the invitation of President Monroe and was escorted on a triumphal tour of the country that lasted a year and has never been matched. He died ten years later.

Montesquieu

"He has always been nearer to the hearts of Americans than any man not of their own people," said Senator Henry Cabot Lodge in an oration delivered in 1904. "Lafayette was the living embodiment of the sympathy of the French people for the cause of the United States. He came because he loved that cause and had faith in it, and so the American people gave faith and love to him." In the First World War, "Lafayette, we are here!" became the motto of the American soldiers who went to fight for France.

Benjamin Franklin remained in Paris until 1785 as America's first Ambassador. After his return to America, old and feeble and in constant pain, he served as one of fifty-five delegates given the task of framing a permanent Constitution of the United States.

The spirit of the French philosopher Montesquieu hovered over their meetings that long hot summer. Time and again he was quoted, by James Madison and Alexander Hamilton and by other delegates. They argued about some of his theories; they dismissed others as outmoded. On one point all the delegates agreed. To produce a workable structure of government, there must be a separation of powers with checks and balances, such as Montesquieu advocated in *The Spirit of the Laws,* to forestall the danger of abuses inherent in a one-man rule.

The decision of the delegates to create a federal government of three branches—the executive office of the Presidency; the legislative made up of the Senate and the House of Representatives; and a judiciary consisting of the Supreme Court and other needed courts—can be traced directly to Montesquieu's influence. The three-part structure might sometimes prove cumbersome and time-consuming, but it provided a sturdy safeguard against tyranny.

In describing democracy, Montesquieu said that to function successfully it must rely on the "civic virtue of the majority of its citizens." Montesquieu, with all his worldly sophistication, was a dreamer, with a dream of a better world. His dream of "civic virtue of the majority of the citizens," with all it implies of integrity, human decency, and justice for all, has never seemed a more practical and realistic necessity.

Bibliography

Balch, Thomas, *THE FRENCH IN AMERICA, during the War of Independence of the United States.* Philadelphia: Porter & Coates. 1891.

Billias, George Athan, Editor, *GEORGE WASHINGTON'S GENERALS.* New York: William Morrow and Company. 1964.

Bonsal, Stephen, *WHEN THE FRENCH WERE HERE.* New York: Doubleday, Doran & Company, Inc. 1945.

Commager, Henry Steele and Richard B. Morris, *THE SPIRIT OF SEVENTY-SIX, The Story of the American Revolution as Told by Participants.* Indianapolis: The Bobbs-Merrill Company, Inc. 1958.

Dupuy, R. Ernest and Trevor N. Dupuy, *THE COMPACT HISTORY OF THE REVOLUTIONARY WAR.* New York: Hawthorn Books, Inc. 1963.

Fay, Bernard, *FRANKLIN, THE APOSTLE OF MODERN TIMES.* Boston: Little, Brown & Company. 1929.

Fleming, Thomas J. *BEAT THE LAST DRUM, The Siege of Yorktown, 1781.* New York: St. Martin's Press. 1963.

Gottschalk, Louis, *LAFAYETTE AND THE CLOSE OF THE AMERICAN REVOLUTION.* Chicago: University of Chicago Press. 1942.

Guizot, M. and Madame Guizot de Witt, *FRANCE.* Vol. V. New York: Peter Fenelon Collier & Son. 1900.

Havens, George R. *THE AGE OF IDEAS, From Reaction to Revolution in Eighteenth Century France.* New York: Henry Holt & Company. 1955.

Hughes, Rupert, *GEORGE WASHINGTON.* 3 vols. New York: William Morrow & Company. 1927.

Lancaster, Bruce and J. H. Plumb, *THE AMERICAN HERITAGE BOOK OF THE REVOLUTION.* New York: Dell Publishing Company. 1963.

Larrabee, Harold A, *DECISION AT THE CHESAPEAKE.* New York: Clarkson N. Potter. 1964.

Latzko, Andreas, *LAFAYETTE.* New York: Doubleday, Doran & Company, Inc. 1936.

Lewis, Charles Lee, *ADMIRAL DE GRASSE AND AMERICAN INDEPENDENCE.* Annapolis, Maryland: U. S. Naval Institute. 1945.

Padover, Saul, *LIFE AND DEATH OF LOUIS XVI.* New York: Taplinger Puplishing Company. 1963.

Richard, Pierre, *LA VIE PRIVÉE DE BEAUMARCHAIS.* Paris: Librairie Hachette. 1951.

Scheer, George F. and Hugh F. Rankin, *REBELS AND REDCOATS.* Cleveland and New York: The World Publishing Company. 1957.

Tournquist, Karl Gustav, *THE NAVAL CAMPAIGNS OF COUNT DE GRASSE DURING THE AMERICAN REVOLUTION.* Philadelphia: Swedish Colonial Society. 1942.

Trevelyan, George Otto, *THE AMERICAN REVOLUTION.* New York: David McKay Company, Inc. 1964.

Van Doren, Carl, *BENJAMIN FRANKLIN.* New York: The Viking Press. 1938.

Whitridge, Arnold, *ROCHAMBEAU.* New York: The Macmillan Company. 1965.

ROCHAMBEAU. A Commemoration by the Congress of the United States of America, Prepared by DeB. Randolph Keim. Washington, D.C.: Government Printing Office. 1907.

CORRESPONDENCE OF GENERAL WASHINGTON AND COMTE DE GRASSE, edited by Institut Français. Washington, D.C.: U. S. Printing Office. 1931.

Index

DATE DUE

MAR 24 70	MR 2 8'83		
JUL 23 70			
APR 5 70			
MAR 1 '72			
MAR 8 '72			
FEB 12 73			
FEB 21 73			
MAR 2 '73			
APR 4 '73			
FEB 14 '74			
MAR 14 '74			
FEB 25 '75			
MAY 11 '77			
OC 25 77			
OC 31 '77			
DE 2'80			
OC 14 '81			
MR 15'83			
GAYLORD			PRINTED IN U.S.A.